Between the Swastika

and the Bear

A Polish Memoir

1925-1948

Andrew D. Jurkowski

Lisa Wright

ISBN-13: 9781934199282

Cover design: Arlene Cook & Lisa Wright

Book layout: Lisa Wright

Editors: Arlene Cook & Réanne Hemingway-Douglass

Photographs courtesy of Andrew Jurkowski

Image page 46 courtesy Wikimedia commons

Maps by Ken Morrison

1.3mp

Published by Cave Art Press, Anacortes, WA, 98221

An imprint of Douglass, Hemingway & Co., LLC

CaveArtPress.com

Cave
Art
Press

Table of Contents

Foreword   5

Family Tree   8

Maps   9

PART I   1885 - 1939

1. My Parents   12

2. My Grandfather and Family   23

3. My Childhood   34

4. Rural Life   46

5. Grabonog and Pudliszki   59

PART II   1939 - 1945

6. The Invasion   67

7. The Occupation's Early Days   76

8. Life Under the Germans   86

9. The Last Days of the Nazis   124

PART III   1945 - 1949

10. The Communists Take Over   134

11. Polish Army Officer Candidate Training   138

12. Labor Camp   145

13. Escape from Poland   151

14. Berlin   157

15. Walking to Freedom   164

16. Working for the U.S. Army   169

17. My Family's Life in Communist Poland   183

PART IV   1949 - 2017

18. Welcome to America   191

19. Living the American Dream   196

20. The Leland Sanatorium and After   199

Appendix: Guide to Polish Pronunciation   206

Acknowledgements   209

Foreword

While visiting my husband's family in Michigan a few years ago, I was showing off my new laptop to my father-in-law, Andrew Jurkowski. Andrew was born in western Poland in 1925 and he came to America as a displaced person in 1948. Thinking he might be interested to see images of his boyhood home, I navigated to the small town of Krobia through the magic of Google Street View and proudly said, "This looks like the market square."

"Very nice," Andrew replied. "Look, right there is the *Ratusz*, the City Hall. That's where the Gestapo lined up their prisoners and shot them in front of the public assembly. We had to load the bodies onto trucks and dump them into a mass grave in the cemetery. Some of the people weren't even dead. They were still choking on their own blood."

Andrew's matter-of-fact account of this atrocity shocked me. The contrast between technology's effortless display of a tranquil Polish hamlet and the horror of mass murder heightened my reaction.

Andrew's sons had grown up hearing stories like this one, but it was new to me. I thought Andrew's memories of life in rural Poland before, during, and shortly after World War II deserved to be collected, preserved, and ideally, shared with a broader audience. This book is based on many hours of recorded interviews with Andrew. We began with his recollections of the German invasion and his life under Nazi occupation. He had just as many stories about the immediate post-war period, when Poland was taken over by the Communists and he saw no alternative but escape to the West as a young man of twenty. More pleasant accounts of his childhood in the vanished world of pre-war Poland were a welcome relief from the nightmares of invasion and occupation. As I heard more of Andrew's stories, I began to see them as living history.

This book is an eyewitness account of events that occurred eighty years ago in a provincial society that has largely vanished. Andrew was fourteen when the Nazis invaded his country, and he is among the last of his generation still alive to describe his experiences. While the geopolitical implications of World War II might have been lost on a schoolboy, Andrew's personal experience of war and its aftermath have remained with him all his life. His narrative is the account of a single life within the larger Polish experience. His individual story is unique, but the hardship and horror he and his family endured reflect the universal suffering of subjugated people everywhere.

Along his journey, Andrew met with brutality and evil but also with kindness and compassion. He has tried to live in accordance with his grandfather's philosophy: we show gratitude to our Creator by helping one another regardless of nationality or religion. This conviction resonates throughout Andrew's experiences and illuminates this account.

Lisa Wright
Anacortes, Washington
August, 2017

I suppose most people have nostalgia for times gone by and perhaps they revisit the scenes of their youth. War and occupation have erased my past so thoroughly that only my memories remain, and this book serves as my return visit. I wanted to tell my story so that it does not vanish with me.

I am thankful I could come to this great country.
I hope it stays that way.

Andrew Jurkowski
Prudenville, MI
August, 2017

Lisa and Andrew, 2017

8

Family Tree

A guide to Polish pronunciation may be found in the appendix.

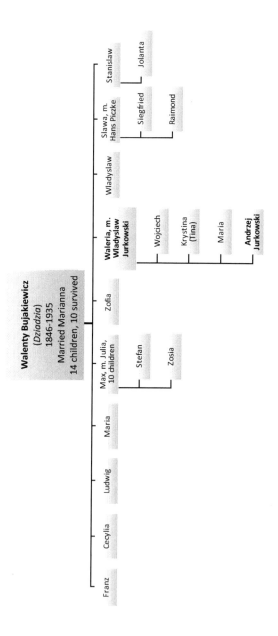

Maps

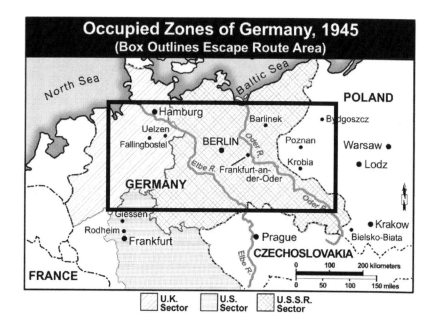

Occupied Zones of Germany, 1945
(Box Outlines Escape Route Area)

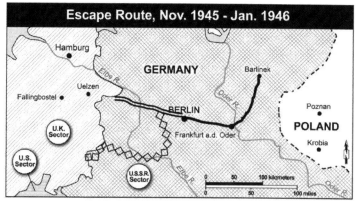

Escape Route, Nov. 1945 - Jan. 1946

Stage 1: Train to Berlin; Nov. 1945

Stage 2: Train from Berlin toward Uelzen, Dec. 1945

Stage 3: On foot to the U.K. Sector; Dec.-Jan. 1945-6

PART I

1885 - 1939

1. My Parents

Waleria Bujakiewicz and Wladyslaw Jurkowski

I was born in rural Poland in 1925. My name in Polish is Andrzej Jurkowski. I was called Andreas when the Nazis controlled my life and I have been called Andrew since I came to America.

I grew up in the small Polish town of Krobia, about fifty miles southwest of the city of Poznan and a hundred miles east of the German border. When I was born, Poland had been independent for only seven years, since the end of World War I. For over a hundred years before independence, Poland had been partitioned among the neighboring great powers of Russia, Austria, and Germany, with Germany controlling the part of western Poland where I grew up. My family was ethnically Polish, but my mother's father, Walenty Bujakiewicz, earned military honors serving with Kaiser Wilhelm's cavalry, and three of my uncles fought for Kaiser Wilhelm II in World War I.

My father and uncles were Polish nationalists, and they worked and fought for the independent Poland that was united under Marshal Pilsudski in 1918. However, my grandfather Walenty always regretted the end of German rule. He said Poland was too disorganized to survive on its own and that it needed Germany's support to avoid being reconquered by Russia.

Eastern Poles were suspicious of Russia's desire to reclaim Polish territory, while Western Poland voluntarily retained a large German influence. In the 19th century, the German government advocated settling colonists in western Poland, and, after independence, Poland's leader, Marshal Pilsudski, encouraged the German colonists to remain. He described them as honorable citizens and good farmers. Many colonists did stay, particularly in the area where I grew up, and they began to assimilate with the upper-class Polish landowners who owned estates around us. Most middle and upper class Poles, including my family, spoke both Polish and German. The Poles were generally Roman Catholic, while the German colonists were a mix of Lutheran and Catholic. There was little ethnic or religious strife in our region, although, as might be expected, there was some resentment among a few of the Polish laborers who worked for German landowners. On the whole, relationships between the Poles and the German colonists were friendly and cooperative, at least until Germany started preparing for another European war and both governments began using propaganda to inflame nationalist feelings.

*   *   *

My father, Wladyslaw, was born in 1882 to Josefat and Dorota Jurkow-ski. Wladyslaw was the second of their five children. His mother, Dorota, died young. Wladyslaw's father, Josefat, was indulgent and had enough money to spoil his motherless children. Wladyslaw and his older brother Roman grew up to be stylish young men who hung around with a fast crowd, drinking in pubs and traveling to nightclubs and cabarets in nearby cities. Wladyslaw was interested in fashion and often said that he hated to see people walking around in shabby or poorly fitting clothes. Josefat wanted his son have a proper start in life, so he offered to pay for Wladyslaw's training at a famous Jewish tailoring shop in Berlin and then set him up in business. In return, Wladyslaw had to promise to quit drinking and settle down to raise a family.

Josefat hired a matchmaker who suggested a union between Wladyslaw and Waleria, one of the five daughters of Walenty Bujakie-wicz, a well-to-do livestock dealer and farmer who lived nearby. Walenty was not in favor of the proposed marriage. He told Josefat that his son was a drunk who would never change. Josefat declared that Wladyslaw had promised to quit drinking. Walenty replied, "Sure, he will keep his vow, just like priests keep their vows. You can't change a drunk." In spite of Walenty's misgivings, the matchmaking went ahead, and Waleria Bujakiewicz was introduced to Wladyslaw Jurkowski in 1908.

Waleria was the sixth of ten children. She was a lively girl of twenty-two when she met Wladyslaw, and like everyone in *Dziadzia's* family, she spoke fluent German and had many friends among the German residents in our area. After finishing grammar school, Waleria had spent several years at a technical institute learning dressmaking. She then went to work for a wealthy German woman who lived on a nearby estate. In addition to employing Waleria as a private seamstress, the lady employed a fashion consultant for herself and her daughters. The consultant gave them advice on gracious living—how they should dress, what the new styles were, and how to hold elegant dinner parties. Waleria lived in their mansion, sewed to their direction, and made a good living. Sadly, her employer contracted tuberculosis, a common and incurable disease in Europe even among wealthy people at that time. Waleria traveled with her employer to Zurich, Switzerland and stayed with her until she passed away.

Around the time she met my father, Waleria received a marriage proposal from one of her cousins. This was before World War I, when Polish nationalists were speaking out strongly against German rule. This cousin was a member of a group openly calling for Polish independence. Someone warned him that German soldiers were coming to arrest him, so he took a train to the coast and fled to South America. He knew Waleria was a spirited young woman, so he wrote and proposed to her, inviting her to join him in Brazil. Waleria obtained a passport without telling her father, but one of her sisters tipped him off and Walenty forbade her to go.

Walenty realized that it was time for Waleria to get married. Walenty agreed that she could marry Wladyslaw Jurkowski after he finished his tailoring training, and the young people became formally engaged.

      *   *   *

Wladyslaw spent two years learning his trade in Berlin and Vienna. Once his training was completed, he came back to Krobia, married Waleria, and opened his own tailor shop. The business started slowly and civilian life was interrupted by World War I and the fight for Polish independence. My father was a captain in the Polish forces fighting for independence, and couldn't keep a close eye on the business, but things improved in the economic boom that followed these events.

Wladyslaw vowed that his customers would always look "first class." He catered to wealthy customers including the Polish nobility and rich German estate owners. His prices were high because his material and workmanship were of the best quality. The business flourished and Wladyslaw employed as many as six men to sew for him.

One time, a German estate owner came in wearing a poorly cut striped suit. He asked Wladyslaw, "How do I look?"

Wladyslaw replied, "You look like a monkey!" His insolence angered the German man, but Wladyslaw showed his customer how the other tailor had cut the suit so poorly that the fabric was pulled out of shape to force the stripes to meet evenly at the seams. Wladyslaw tugged at the shoulder seam and the whole sleeve fell off. There wasn't enough fabric to recut the suit, but Wladyslaw convinced the man to buy a properly tailored suit, and he became a satisfied customer.

Wladyslaw's wealthy clientele could afford his high prices, although they didn't always pay their bills on time. Middle-class people rarely came into his shop. When they did, Wladyslaw showed them various fabrics and told them he'd sew whatever they could afford. The tailoring and workmanship would be just as good, although the cloth wouldn't be as fine. Unlike the nobility, middle-class people were more careful to buy what they could afford and they didn't run up bills they couldn't pay.

*   *   *

I was the youngest of Wladyslaw and Waleria's four children. My brother Wojciech was the oldest. He was born in 1915. My sister Krystina (Tina) came next in 1916. Another sister, Anna, was born in 1917. My sister Maria arrived in 1919, and I came last, in 1925. Anna died of a fever three months after she was born. Our family lived next door to a doctor, who came right away when Anna got sick. In those days, people thought teething could cause an infection and fever and I was told that's why Anna died. My father, who adored all his children, went crazy with grief at Anna's death.

When I was born, Father gathered my brother and sisters and said, "Okay, kids, you have another brother. What should we name him? I like the name Andrzej." Andrzej is Andrew in English.

Wojciech said, "Why did you ask us? It sounds like you've already decided."

Father said, "Well, you can pick his middle name."

"Okay, I like the name Desidariusz."

My sisters said, "We think he should be named after his two grandfathers, Josefat and Walenty."

Father said, "No, no. Two names are plenty." So I was called Andrzej Desidariusz. My sisters were Krystina Maria and Maria Magdalena. At that time in Catholic Poland, most names were based on the saint whose feast day was near the baby's birthday, and almost all the girls were named after the Blessed Virgin Mary as well. Most people also used nicknames of varying degrees of formality, and there's a common Polish saying, "It's an unloved child who has no nickname." My brother Wojciech was called Wojtek, while my sisters were Tina and Misha. My family nickname was Jendrek.

*   *   *

When I was small, we lived in an apartment over my father's shop in Krobia. It was on the main road, and the streetcar ran right past our door. Our apartment shared a wall with the building next door. We lived on one side and one of our many cousins lived on the other side. The front of the downstairs shop had shelf after shelf of different fabrics, all lined up in rows, from the finest and most expensive wools and linens to cotton and canvas, and there was a large workroom in the back. The business did well enough that Father could afford to hire a country girl to work as a maid and helper for Mother. Her name was Kasia, and though our immediate family fortunes changed, she stayed with our extended family for many years.

In the early 1920's, Father's tailoring business was so profitable that he and Mother had enough money to travel for pleasure. He once took Mother to a cabaret show in Breslau where they saw can-can girls. Later, when my sister Tina heard about it, she was shocked. She said, "Mother! You went to that wicked place to see the naked girls?"

Mother said, "Well, I learned more about life outside Krobia. There was nothing wrong with going to the cabaret. I liked hearing the band play, and the show was just girls flipping up their skirts, showing their legs, and shaking their bottoms at stupid men." Mother never found out that some of those men were going with the girls into the back rooms after the show.

*   *   *

Father began to have trouble with his business by the middle of the 1920s. Germany was struggling to pay the reparations awarded to the victors of World War I under the Treaty of Versailles. This led to an economic decline that spread across Europe. People everywhere had trouble paying their bills and debts began piling up. Father worried a great deal about his family and business and he resumed drinking with his no-good friends. He loaned them money in the hope they would bring him more business, but they never did. When Father couldn't afford to pay our maid Kasia any more, she moved out to my grandfather Walenty's farm and worked there.

In 1929, when I was four years old, Mother got a message from one of our cousins that Father had been taken ill. He had been out on a spree somewhere and instead of coming home, he had gone to his father's house all the way across town. I wanted to see him, so I sneaked out from the house without permission and ran all the way to my grandfather's place. Just as I got there, I saw a bus coming down the street. I thought it was far away, so I ran right in front of it and it almost hit me. Father happened to be looking out the window. He ran out to pick me up, bawled me out, and then he hugged me and kissed me. "Now run back to your mama," he said. Then he changed his mind. "No, wait, I better take you back myself," and we walked back home together.

Mother was furious and scolded both of us. Father didn't wait around for a lecture, but waved goodbye and went back to his father's house. That night at midnight, my cousin came and told us that Father was dying. The doctor was already at his side when we got there. I remember being fascinated with the little valise holding the medical instruments. The doctor said there was nothing he could do—Father was dying from a heart attack and we could only wait until he passed away.

We went into the bedroom where I saw Father resting on the bed. He was still semi-conscious and my mother gave him a lit candle to hold. That was the tradition in those days—the dying person would hold the candle for as long as he or she could manage, then someone would take it and hold it nearby. The candle was supposed to keep the soul within its light and lead it through the darkness that was all around. We knelt and Mother led us in prayer. When we finished the rosary and the litany, we all kissed Father and went into the other room. On his deathbed, Father had the nerve to ask Mother to promise never to remarry, but to stay with their children. That seemed unfair to me, but Mother never did remarry.

Sadly, Father's business had so many creditors that government agents were required to confiscate his assets after his death. Mother used to say that Father died with more debts than hairs on his head. I remember a man visiting Mother before the government removal men were to come, and he said, "*Pani** Waleria, you need to conceal some of the shop's fabric before tomorrow morning, so you can sell it later and live off the proceeds. The government agents are required to confiscate all your possessions because your husband left so many debts. Everything must go, even your furniture — the dining room table, the chairs, the dishes. You are allowed to keep only your clothing and your beds. We will sell everything else to reimburse your creditors."

Mother hid as much of the best woolen material as she could in our beds. This was fabric that had come from the famous textile manufacturing city of Bielsko. We slept with it hidden under our sheets. The cloth was of such high quality that when Mother took it out of our beds and shook it, the wrinkles dropped right out. She sold it later to help provide for us.

      *   *   *

---

*Pan and *Pani* are Polish honorifics used by everyone. They mean sir and madam, or gentleman and lady.

Father's father, *Dziadzia* (Grandfather) Josefat, helped our family a little, but he didn't have much to share. He had remarried after *Babcia* (Grandmother) Dorota's death, and his second wife was not interested in supporting the children and grandchildren from Josefat's first marriage. My father had three younger sisters whom the stepmother passed along to her sister-in-law, Antonia, to raise. Aunt Antonia and her sister had been born in Georgia, in the Caucasus. Their Polish father had been exiled there by the czar for political activity in the 1880's and his daughters eventually repatriated to Krobia. Antonia was a beautiful woman, tall and slender. She and her sister often spoke wistfully about their childhood home. They always regretted having to exchange the picturesque mountains and vineyards of Georgia for the flat farmlands of western Poland.

Dziadzia Josefat would tell Mother, "Waleria, when you come from Mass on Sunday, stop and see me with your children." His second wife was so tight with her money that she knew every egg her hens laid, but somehow *Dziadzia* Josefat managed to set aside a few eggs for us. Mother always had us wear clothes with big pockets when we visited after Mass, and *Dziadzia* Josefat usually slipped us a couple of eggs when his wife wasn't looking. I realize now that the experience of his stepmother's meanness was one of the reasons Father made Mother promise that she would never remarry.

My father's elder brother, Roman, also tried to help us. He had a farm and he would occasionally give us a sack of wheat. Mother would take it to the mill and have it ground for flour. That wasn't enough to sustain us, so it was a blessing when, in 1929, Mother's father, *Dziadzia* Walenty, invited us to move into his farmhouse outside Krobia.

Andrzej at age four, with two unidentified women

2. My Grandfather and Family

My grandfather, Walenty Bujakiewicz

My mother's father, *Dziadzia* Walenty Bujakiewicz, was a successful farmer who lived on the outskirts of Krobia. He owned much of his own land and rented even more from the Catholic Church. *Dziadzia* was a well-respected member of his community, with a reputation as a good businessman who was outspoken about politics and religion. He was born in 1846 and lived to the age of eighty-nine. His Catholic ancestors had settled in western Poland after fleeing Lutheran Sweden during the European religious wars of the mid-1600's. Although *Dziadzia* spoke fluent German, and had been awarded medals and an order of merit for his service in the German cavalry under Kaiser Wilhelm I, he was Polish through and through. Nevertheless, he often stated that the Polish people had been better off under German rule than after Poland became independent at the end of World War I. He said, "When Germany governed Poland, we didn't fear the Russians to our east. Kaiser Wilhelm always treated us well. We could be as Polish as we wanted. We had freedom of religion — we could be Lutheran, Catholic, Jew, or whatever, and Germany still protected us."

Dziadzia Walenty's wife, my *Babcia* (grandmother) Marianna, died before I was born. She had been a beautiful woman, with a lovely complexion which all her daughters were fortunate to inherit. Marianna bore fourteen children, prompting people to joke that *Dziadzia* was trying to have a kid for every month of the year. She eventually died from tuberculosis of the bones, which is not surprising after so many pregnancies. Her oldest daughter, my outspoken Aunt Cecilia, often made pointed remarks about the shame of killing women by forcing them to have too many children. We kids were not supposed to listen to such talk, but we overheard it anyway.

Ten of Walenty and Marianna's fourteen children, five boys and five girls, lived to adulthood. Two of their sons were on their own, raising families and working as livestock dealers, farmers, and butchers. *Dziadzia's* oldest son, Franz, was estranged from his father and had moved to Berlin. Three daughters had married, including my mother. Two unmarried sons and two unmarried daughters still lived on the farm with *Dziadzia*. In spite of this, he managed to find space in the farmhouse for us. We moved into two rooms upstairs where there was a kitchen and combined living room and bedroom for the five of us — Mother, Wojciech, Tina, Maria, and me.

*   *   *

Out of natural authority, as much as the fact that we now lived under his roof, *Dziadzia* became the patriarchal figure of my life. He had strong beliefs that he imparted to me, and they have stayed with me all my life.

Dziadzia firmly believed his education had helped him become a success, and he made sure all ten of his children finished grammar school. The local grammar school was run by the government and provided free classes through Grade 7. Beyond grammar school, *Dziadzia* paid for each of his children to receive vocational or military training. To his grandchildren, *Dziadzia* stressed the study of foreign languages, particularly German, because it was so widely spoken in our area. *Dziadzia* would lecture us, "Listen, we live between two powerful countries, Germany and Russia, and we have to know their languages. I hope you will study French too, but German is the most important language for you to learn. The time will come when you will need it, because remember, Germany is only a hundred miles away."

Dziadzia had a deep faith in God. When the church bells rang each evening, he led our family in formal prayers — the rosary, the litany, and vespers — as we listened to the owls calling from the church tower. Sometimes *Dziadzia* slipped from Polish into German and because I was a tired little kid, I would fall asleep. He would catch me and say, "Wake up, you little rascal!"

I would reply, "But *Dziadzia*, you were talking in German." He invariably responded that God understood all languages.

Dziadzia was disappointed by the venality of the local priests. He thought they should be out in the community helping the poor and teaching people to be good by their examples — living virtuous lives of service instead of sitting in their mansions playing cards and drinking wine. *Dziadzia* rebuked the Cardinal of Poznan, telling him, "In the past, the chalices of our church were made of wood and the priests were made of gold. These days, the chalices are golden and the priests are made of wood." *Dziadzia's* blunt criticism was unacceptable. After his harsh words, the Cardinal refused to allow the local Church officials to sell him any more land. The estate managers even withdrew land that *Dziadzia* was renting. When people around Krobia asked why his farm was getting smaller, *Dziadzia* told them what he had said to the Cardinal, and that made the churchmen even angrier.

My aunts said, "Father, why are you always causing problems?"

He said, "I'm not causing any problems. I told the truth and the priests didn't like it. I hear you girls are ashamed of what I said. That's wrong. We are put on this earth to help one another and to be kind. There is only One who will judge me, and nobody else."

*   *   *

When my family moved to *Dziadzia's* farm in 1929, five people already lived there—*Dziadzia*, my two unmarried aunts, Zofia and Maria, who kept house for their father, and my two bachelor uncles, Ludwig and Wladyslaw. Ludwig worked for *Dziadzia* as a butcher. Wlady was a hard worker who took over management of the farm as *Dziadzia* grew older.

Ludwig and Wlady, along with their brother Stan, had all served in the German army in World War I. Ludwig was captured by the Russians and sent deep into Siberia. He was in Kamchatka when the war ended, and he tried to get on a ship headed to San Francisco. Unable to obtain a U.S. visa, he worked his way back to Krobia, but he never recovered from the war and became a hopeless alcoholic. He would give my sister Maria whatever money he had and tell her to run to the shop and bring him a bottle of spirits. Then he would sit and drink it. Maria would be upset with him and plead, "Uncle Ludwig, don't do it! You know how unhappy it makes *Dziadzia* when you get drunk. Try and wait one day. You can do it tomorrow instead."

Ludwig would reply, "I know, I know, this is terrible. But I need something to help me today." Maria's pleading was to no avail, and Ludwig was often incapacitated.

Ludwig was mostly a kind and helpful man, but he teased Maria because he knew how sensitive she was. He made little bleating sounds at her after he slaughtered a calf or a lamb, and then poor Maria couldn't eat it. My aunts would scold him, "You big bum, stop being so mean to her!"

Ludwig would answer, "She needs to get over it. Worse things happen in life." If they were skinning rabbits, he would say, "Meow, meow," and again Maria couldn't eat. Even late in their lives, my sister Tina would tease Maria about her squeamishness.

*　　　　　　　　*　　　　　　　　*

Stan and Wlady also fought for Germany in World War I. They were captured together in 1916 at the battle of Verdun. The family in Krobia heard nothing from them for months and everyone thought they had been killed. The two men had no money after their release from prison camp at the end of the war, so they walked all the way home from France to Poland.

My uncles' experiences in World War I led them to a pessimistic view of Poland's future. Uncle Stan told me, "Remember my words. The time will come when we will be betrayed. When the next war starts, Russia will take Poland back. They hate us for being a separate country and they will make us pay."

I said, "What are you talking about? That can't happen."

"No," he said. "Listen to what I'm telling you. When the Russians come again, and they will, you better get your ass away from here, because there will be fifty years of occupation. I tell you, there will be atrocities."

Being a kid, I didn't take him seriously. But later, when the war ended and Poland fell under Soviet domination, I remembered Uncle Stan's words.

Uncle Stan in WWI uniform

Stan and another of my uncles, Maximillian, lived on their own farms near *Dziadzia's* farm. Like his father, Max dealt in cattle and sheep, buying livestock from farmers, fattening the animals, then selling them to processors all over northern Poland and Germany. Also like his father,

Max fathered a large family. He and his wife, my Aunt Julia, had ten children. Julia was a petite woman, so small and demure that she was nicknamed *Podruszniczka,* after a tiny forest mushroom that grows under fallen leaves. Despite her size, when Julia told her boys to do something, they jumped right on it. I was close to two of Max and Julia's younger children, Zosia and Stefan. Zosia was a petite and pretty girl like her mother, while her brother Stefan was just the opposite. He worked as a butcher and was a strong, husky man, tough as a rock from working with large farm animals. He ate three raw eggs every morning, and whenever he butchered a steer, he would take a cup and drink some of the blood right out of the bucket while it was still hot and foamy.

My fifth uncle, Franz, was the oldest of *Dziadzia's* children. He was the black sheep of the family, and preferred drinking and carousing to work. When *Dziadzia* finally refused to repay any more of his debts, Franz moved to Berlin and we never heard from him again.

Max and Stan acted as the heads of the family after *Dziadzia's* death in 1935, until Max died in 1937 during emergency surgery for an undiagnosed hernia.

*   *   *

In addition to my five uncles, I also had four aunts. Two of them, Cecylia and Slawa, had married German citizens. Zofia and Maria never married and they lived with us on *Dziadzia's* farm.

Aunt Cecylia was *Dziadzia's* oldest daughter. She was a wonderful person who loved life and did everything with her whole heart, even after her husband and baby both died of tuberculosis. Cecylia's marriage to a German man had given her *Reichsdeutsch* citizenship, meaning she was considered legally German rather than Polish. She never remarried and spent many years working as the household manager for a family of German nobility at their manor house in Pomerania. A hard worker and a wheeler-dealer who saved her money, Cecylia purchased her employers' manor outright when they returned to Germany after Polish independence, and she became a prominent local citizen. She loved music and she was a sponsor of the civic opera company in Bydgoszcz. She never missed a performance, traveling to town in her carriage pulled by a pair of fine horses. I fell in love with opera after Aunt Cecylia took me to see *I, Pagliacci* when I was eleven.

Cecylia had a great sense of humor. Most of my aunts and uncles were tall and slender, while Cecylia was short and stout. She would laugh at her figure and say, "Well, a real woman needs a chest to breathe with and a bottom to sit on." She loved practical jokes. In those days, we celebrated our saint's feast day like a birthday, and Cecylia always sent a box of special *pączki* (jam-filled Polish doughnuts) to the farm for Valentine's Day—the feast day of *Dziadzia's* patron saint. She would invariably conceal shredded cellophane in one special doughnut and arranged with her sisters to serve that one to *Dziadzia*, just to make everyone laugh.

Cecylia was an excellent card player and she held weekend card parties that were renowned for their elaborate hospitality, particularly her fashionable and original hors d'oeuvres. Cecylia's guests always included the local priests, to whom she would say, "Now, if you don't want to play for money, that's fine with me, but if you want to play for money, you know who you're up against." When the priests teased her about never remarrying, Cecylia laughed and said, "None of you has married, and you're happy enough. I don't need a husband any more than you need a wife! I would be just as happy with a liver sausage!" Then it would be the priests' turn to laugh—and Cecylia would win all their money.

One of the priests once asked, "If you keep taking all our money, who will hear your confession when you are dying?"

Cecylia answered, "What sins do I have to confess? I am a hard-working woman and a widow. I'm not going to hell."

That kind of irreligious remark upset my mother. As the widowed mother of four, Mother had a more authoritarian outlook than Cecylia, and she was more devout in her Catholic faith. Mother would say to Cecylia, "Don't talk like that in front of the children."

Cecylia replied, "Why not? Sooner or later, everyone has to find out how life works."

It was always a party when Cecylia came to visit us in Krobia. She loved young people and she was always fair and honest when she played cards with us. Yet somehow, when she played with the priests and older people, she always won. If people complained, Cecylia said, "If you're stupid, you shouldn't gamble. I get good cards, and that's just the way it goes."

Her sister Zofia once asked her, "Cecylia, it takes good cards to win. How do you always manage to get the good cards?"

Cecylia laughed and replied, "Oh, well, that's another story…"

*   *   *

Dziadzia's second daughter was my Aunt Slawa. She had also married a German man, Hans Pietschke, and they lived in Berlin. Hans was from a family of teachers. He had met Slawa when he and his brother were teaching in Krobia before Polish independence.

After World War I ended, post-war rationing in Germany made life hard for Slawa and her family. In 1922, Slawa wrote to her father describing the shortages. In response, Mother planned a trip to help her sister, and packed two suitcases full of sausages and bacon to take to Berlin. Though black market smuggling to beat taxation and rationing was a way of life across Poland and Germany between the wars, it was also a criminal offense, and Mother risked arrest and possibly jail. She was on her way to catch the train when one of her cousins intercepted her with a warning. Someone had informed the police about her trip and they planned to arrest her at the train station.

Mother returned to *Dziadzia's* house, hid the meat deep in the cellar, and went to visit a neighbor. While she was gone, the police came to search the house. When Mother came back, she saw the cellar doors open and she could hear voices. She closed the doors, locking the men inside, and returned to the neighbor's house. After an hour, she came home and pretended to be very surprised. "What's that racket? Who is in the cellar?"

"We are the police! Let us out!"

Mother opened the door and said "What are you doing in our cellar? You aren't allowed to be here when no one is home." The policemen said they were investigating a report that she was taking food to Berlin to be sold on the black market. They wouldn't reveal the informant. Slawa never got the sausages, but at least Mother wasn't arrested.

Slawa and Hans visited *Dziadzia's* farm every summer with their sons, Siegfried and Raimond. Uncle Hans was a jolly man and we all loved him. He had a strong German accent when he spoke Polish, so it

was easy to tease him, but he always laughed it off. Siegfried and Raimond were rambunctious boys who ran around with the sons of the local German colonists, as well as with my brother Wojciech and me. *Dziadzia* always told his German grandsons that when they were in Poland,
they had to speak Polish. They would say, "But the other kids will laugh
at us when we make mistakes!"

Dziadzia would reply, "The Polish kids make mistakes when they
speak German. You should be teaching each other. That's how everybody learns."

Aunt Cecylia

3. My Childhood

Andrzej, age twelve

When my family moved to *Dziadzia's* farm, Mother felt that it wasn't fair for us to be completely dependent on her father's charity. Even though it had been fifteen years since she had stopped working, she still had a reputation as a fine seamstress, so she began sewing for a living again. She sometimes left us kids in the care of our aunts and uncles for several months at a time, while she traveled to distant estates and sewed for wealthy ladies.

We moved to the farm when I was four years old, in 1929. When I was five, I started at the grammar school in Krobia. Wojciech and Tina had finished grammar school by the time I started, so I walked to school with my sister Maria, and later with friends. The public grammar school went from Grade 1 through Grade 7 and attendance was free. We studied math, writing, Polish and foreign languages, and science. Science was divided into biology and physical science. We also had art and history. History was very hard for me. I could never remember all the dates, so I cheated on an exam. I wrote the first letter of the event and the date on my fingernails. The teacher noticed and yelled, "Oh Lord! Go wash your hands!" He sent me home with a note saying I had cheated, which Mother had to acknowledge and return. Mother made me kneel on two sacks of dry beans and pray the rosary. The embarrassment and disgrace of being caught was as bad as the pain of the punishment and I didn't try cheating again.

Our school day started at 8 a.m. and ended at 4 p.m. Boys and girls were in the same classes, but we marched into the building in two separate lines. We had two hours of free time in the middle of the day, from noon until 2 p.m. We ate the lunches we'd brought from home, and then we could get help with our lessons or play soccer.

Our school had all kinds of students—Germans and Poles, Catholics, Protestants, and Jews—all mixed in together. Every morning, each class said prayers. At the start of my first year, our teacher said, "Our class has this many Protestant children, this many Jewish children, and this many Catholic children. When we pray each morning, they will say their prayers, and we will say our prayers. Don't you be rude and turn around and gape at them." I was curious and turned around anyway. My Jewish friends, the Bilski boys, were standing respectfully, not moving or even blinking, and up on the wall in front of me was the crucifix of my Catholic faith — shame on me! The teacher caught me looking and gave me a smack. He sent a note home to my mother and she smacked me some more.

After school came chore time. My chore was to sweep the stone courtyard. This area was paved with flat stones and surrounded on three sides by our house, a laundry and storage building, and the stables for the horses. Chickens wandered around and pooped everywhere, so I had to sweep it clean every afternoon. *Dziadzia* and Mother both hated seeing dirt.

After chores, Mother made sure I started my homework. We all ate dinner together. We thanked *Dziadzia*, and he blessed us. Then I would go upstairs and do more schoolwork. Mother was always asking, "Are you up on your work? Are you having any problems?" She would say to my brother, "Wojciech, help him study." Later, when it was dark, we sat a while by the kerosene lamps, then we said our prayers together and went to bed.

In winter, Mother prepared hot water bottles to keep us warm. There was a stove in the bedroom and Mother bought coal when she could afford it, but usually we lit only the kitchen stove. We kept the doors open from the kitchen to the bedroom so it was a little warmer. We also slept under a lot of bedding. On winter mornings, the windows would have beautiful designs on them made from the steam of our breath freezing against the icy glass. On cold mornings, I pulled my clothes under the bedding with me to warm them up as much as I could. Then I dressed and got up. Mother always said, "When your father looks down from heaven, I hope he's happy to see what he did to you kids, how we have to live all together in one cold room."

Sometimes we'd be walking in town with Mother when we saw Father's old cronies approaching. They always quickly crossed the street to walk on the other side. Mother would say, "Ah, *Dzien dobry, Pan* [Good day, sir]. Don't run away from me. I'm not going to ask you for anything. My husband didn't have to die a drunk. He fell for your lies and that's why he left me alone with four little children. And look how successful you have become!" Either their guilty consciences or her sharp words led them to cross the street to avoid her.

*   *   *

My two best friends, the brothers Alfons and Wlady Chudy, lived in the house just down the road from our farmhouse. They were a little older than me. We walked together to school in town every morning and we spent our summers playing in the fields and woods. Alfons and Wlady had a little curly-tailed dog named Foxy who went everywhere with us. In the summer, we swam in the ponds and ditches and caught crawfish under the stones. Once Alfons caught a catfish with his bare hands, and held it up so we could look. The fish's drooping whiskers and gulping mouth reminded us of my grandfather, and we laughed until we were helpless.

In the winter, rain flooded the farm fields and we waited impatiently until it was cold enough for them to freeze over. Once that happened, we could skate for miles. When I was a little kid, my ice skates tied onto my shoes with leather straps, but when I was ten years old, Aunt Zofia gave me a pair of the fancy new style of ice skate that clamped onto the bottoms of my shoes and tightened with a key. We kids were cold, but we loved the freedom and fresh air as we skated for hours. Moving freely under the wide skies was a welcome break from the confinement of home, school, and church.

        *   *   *

Agricultural work ordered rural life in those pre-war days and the various seasons were punctuated by religious festivals. Christmas and Easter were the most important celebrations, but we enjoyed a holiday feast almost every month.

I especially looked forward to the *Wigilia* supper, a special feast on Christmas Eve that is an important occasion for Poles all over the world, even today. Unlike Christmas Day, Christmas Eve is part of the Advent season. Like Lent, Advent is a season of fasting, so no meat is served at the *Wigilia*. Nonetheless, it is a feast of many dishes.

Our *Wigilia* meal did not begin until the first star shone in the sky. We said prayers and exchanged a wafer of holy bread with one another, sharing hugs, kisses, and wishes for happiness. A lighted candle placed in the front window and an extra place at the table were ready to welcome any unexpected visitors. The meal always began with soup made from wild mushrooms that had been picked and dried in the autumn. Then we had fried fish and pierogis stuffed with potatoes and onions or sauerkraut and mushrooms. The table was loaded with mashed potatoes, other vegetables, sauerkraut, and herring. We had a fruit compote for dessert. After the feast, we went to church for midnight Mass.

The Christmas tradition in our area was for Saint Nicholas to visit the house on Christmas Eve, before the *Wigilia* meal. We called him *Gwiazdor* (Star-man), because he came just as the first star began to shine. *Gwiazdor* brought presents, but he also spanked children who had been rude or naughty. He carried a wooden stick wrapped in leather. The ends of the straps hung down and they were wet, so that once I was hit on my rear end, I thought, oh, I don't want to feel that again! The better we had behaved, the better present we received. A child who had misbehaved might be given only a bread roll.

Gwiazdor announced his arrival at our door with jingling bells. He would ask me how many times I had been naughty, what bad things I had done, and if I had been talking back to the grown-ups. I would confess my bad deeds and words, and then I had to apologize in his presence to whomever I had offended. I also had to recite an Our Father and a Hail Mary. Then *Gwiazdor* would say, "I will spank you twice as much next year if you do these things again, because I tell you, I know everything and I don't forget!" We always wondered how *Gwiazdor* knew what we had done. Now I know that the grown-ups told him before he came in. I smile when I look back at these memories, even though I was scared of *Gwiazdor's* whip. I could never figure out why he needed to spank me. I tried hard to be good.

*　　　　　*　　　　　*

I remember the Christmas Eve when I was seven. I was next door at the house of my friends Alfons and Wlady Chudy when we heard the ringing bells that announced *Gwiazdor's* arrival. He stamped his boots and yelled, "Where are those bad boys? Where are Alfons and Wlady?" We all scooted under the big bed with their little dog, Foxy. *Gwiazdor* knew we were there because Foxy was barking. He shouted, "You kids come out of there right now, or I'll move that bed and then I'm going to whip you!"

Alfons and Wlady yelled back, "Oh no you won't! It's too heavy!" Those boys were so sassy! *Gwiazdor* couldn't move the bed, so he reached under it to pull us out. I was terrified. Alfons and Wlady pushed me between them so *Gwiazdor* couldn't catch me. He grabbed at Alfons, but Alfons shoved Foxy right at him and Foxy bit his hand. *Gwiazdor* lost his temper and started hitting at us with his whip. He couldn't quite reach us, so he went around and tried from the other side of the bed. Alfons passed Foxy to Wlady, who shoved Foxy at *Gwiazdor*, and Foxy bit him again! It was a madhouse of yelling and barking.

Pan Chudy came in and said, "Okay, they've had enough." He quieted everybody down and persuaded us to come out from under the bed. I remember being so scared I was shaking. Alfons and Wlady had to kneel, apologize, and beg for forgiveness. *Gwiazdor* looked at me and said, "What are you doing here? Get out of here now! Do you know how to get home?"

"Yes," I said, and ran home as fast as I could.

When I got there, my aunts said, "Why are you so pale and scared? You can't even talk." Aunt Zofia made me tell her the whole story. She said, "Well, that's what you get for not listening. I told you not to go over there because I knew *Gwiazdor* would be starting to make his rounds. You didn't listen and you got what you deserved."

        *   *   *

Every year, after *Gwiazdor's* visit, we ate our *Wigilia* supper. Then we opened presents from under the Christmas tree. In those days, children were usually given clothes—shirts, undershirts, and long johns—sewn by their mothers and aunts. People didn't buy clothes—almost everything was homemade. One year Aunt Zofia gave me slippers that were like Indian moccasins. She had taken the felt from a couple of old hats, wet it, and stretched it out. Then she shaped it like a boot and sewed old leather scraps onto the sole. She lined it with rabbit skins and those moccasins lasted until I outgrew them.

Everyone received caps, gloves, and sweaters. I was always happy to receive knitted socks that came up to my knees to keep me warm when I walked to school. My aunts and mother knit all year round, and they shared a spinning wheel and a sewing machine. They spun and knit sheep's wool, as well as the hair from some angora rabbits that we kept in a special cage. The aunts combed the hair from the rabbits, washed and dried it, and spun it into a fine, fluffy yarn for luxury items.

*　　　　　　　*　　　　　　　*

Easter was another important holiday. Every year toward the end of Lent, *Dziadzia* ordered his son Ludwig to slaughter animals to share with his family and everyone else. Ludwig always grumbled, "Why so much? Everybody should buy their own."

Dziadzia had a large family to support, but he told us all that it was our responsibility to share because we had so much. He said, "My hard work made me wealthy, but God's mercy made it possible." He contributed meat to the convent, to the priests, and to our neighbors. Selfishness was the worst sin *Dziadzia* could think of. He shared more with the people he thought were more deserving, so his hard-working sons got hams and bacons, and the lazy ones got sausages.

Whatever the occasion, *Dziadzia* was happiest when he had his entire family gathered around him — all his children and grandchildren — but I think we all enjoyed the Easter feasts the most. Spring was in the air, and the struggles of winter were behind us. The big farm table held twenty-four people with everyone wedged in together. It was covered with stuffed veal roasts, potatoes, and dozens of hard-boiled eggs. Mother used a little wooden mold to make a lamb out of butter, with peppercorns for eyes, a little sprig of leaf to make a mouth, and a little Easter flag that looked like the flag of Switzerland. It was so cute that no one ever wanted to be the first to cut into it.

*   *   *

On feast days and other religious holidays, many people dressed in traditional folk costumes. In our region of Bizkupiznie, the men's costumes were mostly black, unlike the more colorful costumes from Warsaw and Krakow. The men wore high velvet hats and long, tight-fitting black woolen jackets with a narrow band of cardinal red trim around the collar, along the lapels, and down the front edges, as well as along the pockets. The red color showed they were from an area where most of the land belonged to the Church. The trousers were also black and puffed out just below the knee, where they went into high black boots.

Women's costumes were made of brightly colored silk. The bodices were tightly laced, while the skirts were full and held out by two or three petticoats and covered with silk aprons. The women wore elaborate lace bonnets and most women had a necklace of coral beads. Their black leather shoes had openings up the fronts that showed their black stockings. Although most people wore their costumes only on special occasions, our maid Kasia wore a variation of the regional costume every day. She wore a tight-laced bodice, full skirts and petticoats, and a colorful apron even on hot summer days. When Mother asked if the tight lacing and many layers made her hot, Kasia replied, "No, I'm not hot. This costume belongs to us. It's made of light and beautiful colors, while you are dressed all in black. You look like you're hotter than me."

*   *   *

The folk costumes were generally worn by ethnic Poles like us. My family was Roman Catholic. Our Polish language and traditions, as well as our Catholic faith and practice, were a significant part of our Polish identity. I was surprised when I first learned that non-Catholics, whether they were Lutherans or Jews, also thought of themselves as Polish. The Jews I knew in Krobia had an exotic allure for me, since they spoke other languages in addition to Polish and German, and worshipped in a different way. Jewish settlement in Poland dates back almost 1000 years. Various regimes treated Jews with greater and lesser tolerance, but even after their long history among us, Jews still seemed indefinably foreign.

Many of the homes around Krobia's market square belonged to Jews. The synagogue was right behind the square. I was a curious kid and wanted to attend one of their services. Mother wouldn't allow it. She said, "No, they don't come to our church and we have to respect their church. If you want to know how they pray, go ask *Pan* Zucker." *Pan* Zucker was a Jewish tanner in town who processed the hides Uncle Ludwig brought after butchering a cow or sheep. Ludwig knew a lot about the Jewish religion, and he sang some Hebrew verses for me.

When I was eleven, Mother took me to the funeral of *Pan* Zucker's wife. Mother told me that if I wasn't respectful, or if she heard any laugh-

ing, she would slap me. I believed her, because she slapped me whenever I deserved it, and often when I didn't. I had already heard many
absurd things about Jewish funerals — for example that Jews were buried
in a semi-sitting position so that after death they could get out of the
grave quicker, although it never occurred to me to ask why they would
want to do that. We went to the funeral at the synagogue, and we had to
wash our hands before we went in and after we came out. The cantor
stood by with a towel, and I was quiet because I knew if I made a noise
Mother would slap me and that would have been shameful. I saw *Pani*
Zucker laid out in her casket, propped up on pillows. After the service,
the pillows were taken out and she lay flat, just like a Christian. We followed a professional mourner to the cemetery.

When I was a boy, Aunt Maria told me about a shameful thing she
and her cousin Pelagia had done when they were in their late teens. One
Friday evening during the summer, Maria and Pelagia went to the
nearby home of a Jewish family. Everything was prepared for the Sab-
bath dinner, with candles, fine linens, and an elegantly set table. While
the family was away at the synagogue, the girls tossed a cat through the
open window into the dining room and ran away. Plates were broken,
candles knocked over, and a small fire started. Fortunately, a servant
was there to put the fire out. The girls were afraid their fathers would
find out what they had done and punish them, not only physically, but
by forcing them to make a formal visit to apologize during the middle of
the day so that everyone would hear about of their disgraceful behavior.
Much later, Aunt Maria told me, "I am old now and I am still mortified
by my action. It was a desecration of their faith. I was young and stupid
and I didn't get caught. I still regret what we did."

Maria was lucky *Dziadzia* never found out, because her behavior would have disappointed him. He taught us that actions always spoke louder than words, and being kind to others was the way we should express our gratitude for God's blessings.

Folk costumes of Krobia
(courtesy Wikimedia commons)

4. Rural Life

Haying on Dziadzia's *farm*

The part of Poland where I grew up is called Bizkupiznie, which means "Under the Bishops." Several hundred years ago, the King of Poland gave most of the farmland in the area to the Catholic Church. The Church still owned much of the land around us, although they sometimes sold acreage to local farmers such as *Dziadzia* if they needed funds.

Farming was the primary industry in our area. Agricultural estates surrounded us for thirty or forty miles in every direction. The two estates closest to *Dziadzia's* farm were Chumientki and Pudliszki. The Chumientki estate belonged to the church and the mansion was used as a vacation resort for cardinals, bishops, and high ranking priests from all over Poland. As on many other estates, the fields were leased to tenant farmers. The estate manager told the farmer what crops to grow — usually wheat or rye. The farmer paid rent in money and part of the harvest. The Church sent the grain to their storehouses in Poznan, where it was redistributed to the Catholic-run hospitals and orphanages and to the needy in villages around the region.

The other nearby estate, Pudliszki, was a large-scale agricultural operation. The property included several thousand acres of farmland and forests, as well as a sawmill and a factory that manufactured canned products for export all over Europe. There were hundreds of cold frames for starting vegetables in the spring, and a nursery for propagating young fruit trees. Pudliszki's cannery and factory were renowned for high-quality jams and preserves, as well as hams and sausages, and their products were exported all over Europe.

In the town of Krobia itself, a middle class of merchants and craftsmen provided services and products for the estates and their workers. These people earned their livelihoods from a variety of occupations — as butchers, storekeepers, livestock dealers, and small farmers. They generally owned their own homes or small farms, while the working class people who provided labor for the estates rented cottages from the various estate owners, both Polish and German. The laborers were paid with farm products as well as in cash. Estate laborers usually had their own garden plot and raised small livestock — typically a pig or a few sheep and some chickens or geese — which they fed with the fodder and grain they received as payment from the estate.

*   *   *

Dziadzia's farm was a private holding and not part of an estate. It was on the outskirts of Krobia and included a manor house that sat in its own grounds. From there, *Dziadzia* ran a successful livestock trading business with customers in western Poland and eastern Germany. He bought as much agricultural land as the Church would sell him, and he rented more.

Dziadzia and his sons made good livings trading in livestock. They bought, fattened, and sold cattle, sheep, and pigs. Some of their livestock went to the factory at the Pudliszki estate to be turned into sausages and canned hams that were sold all over Poland and Europe. Some Pudliszki products were even exported to America as part of Poland's reparations for World War I; however by the 1930's, most were exported to Germany, where the government was stockpiling supplies for their growing military. *Dziadzia* had many customers in Germany who had been buying from him since before World War I. They knew his stock was always high quality and they preferred to buy from him because the shipments were always heavier than the weights written on the bills. *Dziadzia* made sure the livestock were well-cared for while in transit. He was furious if animals were left hungry or thirsty, and he fired any workers who neglected them. He would say, "You sure know how to feed your own mouths. The animals need food too!"

Dziadzia grew a variety of crops on his farm, including potatoes, wheat, oats, rye, and sugar beets. The beets were sold to a sugar factory, although some were processed right on the farm. The juice was squeezed out in a press, and then boiled in kettles to concentrate it into molasses syrup. Some of the juice was cooked at a lower heat, so the syrup remained white instead of brown, and this was pressed into sugar cakes in large flat pans. I always liked sugar-making, because I got to nibble on leftover bits.

Every springtime, *Dziadzia* hired laborers from among the people who went from farm to farm looking for work. *Dziadzia* would offer them a verbal contract, saying, "Look, I can give you so many kilos of rye, wheat, and oats. I will pay this much cash, and you'll get meat and sausages when I slaughter in the fall." The laborers were happy with the arrangement, but *Dziadzia* had to worry, because even if the harvest was poor, he still had to pay them. If he didn't, the laborers wouldn't come back the next year. *Dziadzia* was proud of his reputation as a fair and trustworthy employer, and said it was his obligation to pay his workers. He had hired the people, he had promised to pay them, and he always did. His sons knew they would get paid too, although in some years *Dziadzia* would warn them, "Watch out, boys! You'll be paying for your own bread this year, because I have to pay the laborers first. I promised to pay them, but I didn't promise to pay you anything." One year, a drought forced *Dziadzia* to sell off most of his cattle and pigs because he couldn't grow enough fodder for them — but he still managed to pay his laborers.

Temperatures reached 95 degrees in a typical summer. The heat was hard on the workers, although it was good for the crops. Farmers kept a careful eye on the weather so they could harvest during a hot, dry period. When *Dziadzia* predicted a few days of fine weather, he would say, "Boys, tomorrow, early in the morning, we will all go cut the wheat." A workman drove a mechanical reaper pulled by a team of draft horses. Three or four women walked behind the reaper with scythes. They gathered the stalks, tied them into bundles, and then set them up into shocks. At the end of the day, men hitched up wagons, loaded all the shocks, and brought everything into the grain barn. Windows and vents directed any breezes to blow through the barn to keep the grain from getting spoiled by damp or mold, causing the loss of the whole year's work. Hay also needed care to prevent it from spoiling. When the workers cut hay, they pitched it into stacks twenty feet high. Then more hay was spread out over the top of the stack to make a thatched roof that shed rain.

After harvest, *Dziadzia* sold his grain to the mill. The miller paid by the kilo, then ground most of the grain and sold it to other customers. He also ground some grain for our own use, since every household baked its own bread in those days.

The farm traded products for services as well as for money. When we had a butchering, the sausages were shared with everyone—the laborers got some, our uncles' families got some, the nuns and priests got some, and *Dziadzia* gave some to the poor people who lived around him.

Other items could be bought in town. Krobia had a general store, a butcher shop, a couple of tailors and shoemakers, a furrier and a tanner, and a dairy store selling milk, butter, and cheese. The general store sold staples like sugar, candy, herrings in a barrel, small smoked fish, tea, and coffee. The butcher had fresh meat available two or three times a week. He might slaughter a steer on Monday and sell it all by Thursday. Then he might slaughter a pig or a sheep. People ate a lot of mutton and lamb.

We ate well in the pre-war years. The farm had a large garden for winter vegetables such as carrots, potatoes, and cabbages, which we stored in the cellar for winter. *Dziadzia* kept chickens, pigs, and cows for our family's use and the men slaughtered twice a year, in November and in March. *Dziadzia* also kept a large flock of chickens and sold eggs to the market in Krobia. He even had some of the fancy Polish hens, the kind with the crest of ornamental feathers all around their heads. A pigeon loft sat at the top of the barn and Aunt Zofia sometimes turned its inhabitants into my favorite, pigeon pie. Pigeons were a great delicacy and an important food for invalids because they were thought to be particularly easy to digest. Bats lived under the pigeon loft and they zoomed around the farmyard at night, patrolling for insects. One night someone forgot to shut the door to the pigeon loft and an owl got in and killed almost all the pigeons.

*   *   *

Every farm had its own well, along with a cistern for water storage. Our farm had the best water — it was always clear and cold and it never ran low, even in the driest summers. There were some years when our neighbors' wells ran dry, and they had to carry buckets home from our well.

Each morning, we filled buckets with a hand pump, carried them to the cistern, and poured the water into it. The cistern was a fifty-gallon enameled tank with a faucet on the bottom. It stood on a stand in the hallway just outside the kitchen and my aunts drew water from it for cooking and washing.

In the winter, we kept a couple of buckets standing near the stove so the water would warm to room temperature. Getting water from the well was difficult in cold weather. We had to cover the wellhead with bales of straw to keep it from freezing, then pull a couple of the bales off when we needed to pump the water. After World War II, when Stan and

Wlady were running the farm, Stan hooked up a gas-powered pump, but before then, everything was done by hand. Piped city water didn't come to the farm until late in the 1950s.

In my childhood, my family bathed in wooden tubs. My aunts pulled two tubs into the kitchen and drew enough water to fill one of them. They heated it up by adding boiling water from kettles on the stove, and closed off the kitchen so the room got warm. I was the smallest, so I went first. I sat in the empty tub while Mother or an aunt washed me with a bucket of warm water from the other tub. Then the next kid washed after me, with another bucket of warm water added to the tub, and so on. The women followed the kids, and then it was the men's turn, always with more warm water added for each person. We bathed just once a week, although I had to wash my face, neck, and feet every day.

In those days, we used an outhouse for a toilet. People went into the little house out back and did their business, then got out quickly because it stunk. Most people used newspaper for toilet paper. If they didn't have newspaper, they used hay. The women used little flannel cloths when they had their monthly periods. Later, when cotton became available, they sewed little cloth bags and stuffed them with cotton. They buried the soiled cotton in the compost heap, washed the flannels, and hung them on the line. Everywhere you went, you would see the washing lines loaded with narrow cloths. In the winter, my aunts hung the laundry on lines in the attic. We kids always wondered about all those skinny cloth things hanging on the lines. When I asked, Mother said, "You will learn about in due time it. Just forget about it for now."

Most women wore light makeup in those days—just powder and lipstick. Mother didn't wear powder because she said it ruined her complexion. She used an imported French face cream every night, and she and my aunts used fine French face soap instead of homemade soap. The egg-shaped bars were scented with lilac and lily-of-the-valley and wrapped in tissue paper. Mother put the tissues in among folded linens so they smelled nice when the sheets were changed. When it became obvious that war was coming, Mother and her sisters concealed a hundred bars of imported soap under the eaves in the attic. They spent the war years worrying that inspectors would find and confiscate the soap and punish them.

*   *   *

Pan Chudy, the father of my friends Alfons and Wlady, ran a factory that produced vegetable oils with a press. Farmers brought cartloads of flax and sunflower seeds, which the factory processed into cooking oil. A different factory used the fibers in the flax stems to make linen thread. Flax is a tricky crop to grow successfully — the plants need to be dry enough — but not too dry — for the fibers in the stems to be processed and spun into linen thread, while the seeds in their tiny pods need to be ripe without being dried out. Rain at harvest time would ruin everything, so deciding just the right time for harvest was always a challenge for the farmers.

One day, *Pan* Chudy invited us to his factory to watch the process of making flax seed oil. The flax seeds were squeezed in a press, and the oil ran off and was bottled. The leftover seeds were baked over a stove in flat pans. Women stood over them stirring with wooden paddles while the seeds browned. *Pan* Chudy said, "Here boys, you want some candy?" We jumped for it, and he gave us a cake of the cooked seeds. It was very tasty, but it sure made my bowels move!

In addition to flax and sunflower oil, the factory produced oil from poppy seeds. The leftover seed cakes were delicious, and I can still taste their sweetness. But it always made me very sleepy, and I didn't learn why until later when I found out that poppy seeds could be made into narcotics.

*   *   *

I could have used some of those poppy seeds when I was six years old and broke a bone in my right hand. I had been running around in the garden and fell into a hole. There were no X-rays in those days and no anesthetic for a little kid either. The doctor set my hand simply by looking at it and pulling it back to the right position. Then he put on a wooden splint and a plaster cast. The next year, when I was seven, I broke my right wrist, and when I was eight, I broke my right arm. Both of those accidents happened when I tripped and fell while playing jump rope. When I visited the doctor with my third broken bone, he looked at me and said, "What in the hell are you doing? If you break this arm again, I'm going to chop it off right here!" He scared the hell out of me and after that I was very careful and gave up jumping rope.

We were fortunate, because the doctor in our neighborhood was particularly capable. People went to him when they had a temperature, a sore throat, a belly ache, or a similar complaint, and he would come to patients in an emergency.

More serious cases went to one of the two hospitals in our region. They were fifteen and thirty miles away respectively, and were run by Catholic nuns. People went to the hospital by horse and cart, or by sleigh in the winter. We had no health insurance and hospitals depended on the patients to pay their bills. If someone couldn't pay, the nuns bartered with the patient's family. They agreed to a contract for so many eggs, or

chickens, or kilos of grain. They calculated how much the hospital service cost, the price of the chickens or whatever at the time the patient
was admitted to the hospital, and the patient signed an agreement. It
was a good system and it provided the hospital with the food supplies
they needed. The hospital had its own kitchens and bakery. A butcher
came to process the livestock, and nuns took bartered grain to the mill.
The Church subsidized the hospitals with supplemental cash and food
from tithes paid by parishioners.

The nuns also helped people who were too poor to pay. They
would negotiate with the family, saying, "We know you don't have any
income or any goods to barter. You can pay by working for us. You can
prepare your patient's food at home and bring it to him, and you can cut
wood or work in the laundry or sweep the drive."

The nurses were all nuns. They assisted the doctors and did all the
other hospital work—sterilizing instruments and working in the laundry and kitchen. I became friends with one of the nursing sisters, Sister
Josefina, who told me stories about her experiences. She had worked for
several years in a hospital in the coal mining city of Rybnik. The miners
were heavy drinkers, and they would come to the emergency depart-
ment when they were blind drunk. Sister Josefina told me, "I'll never
forget the time a man came in with appendicitis. He was completely
drunk. We kept him waiting for a little bit, until the doctor said, 'We
can't wait any longer. Give him the ether and put him to sleep, and I'll
operate.'" Sister Josefina was the anesthetist, and she also assisted the
doctor by handing him the various instruments. After the patient was
unconscious, the doctor made his first incision, and the drunk miner
woke up with a BANG! He ripped away the ether mask, the draperies,
and the instruments, and he tried to run out of the operating room. The

staff were terrified because his belly was wide open and his insides were coming out. They wrestled the patient back onto the table and gave him a lot more ether so the doctor could finish the operation. Ether was dangerous for those hard drinkers. It just made them more drunk without knocking them out.

Dr. Walentowski was a famous surgeon in our area and people came to him from all over. His parents were German colonists who had stayed in Poland after independence. He was a good surgeon, especially for those days, and he was also very self-assured. Sister Josefina told me stories about him, too. Dr. Walentowski did not like his nurses to speak to him even if he picked up the wrong instrument. She cautioned him the first time she assisted him, saying, "Doctor, don't touch that, you need the other one."

Dr. Walentowski yelled at her, "God damn it! Don't tell me what to do! I'm the surgeon here, and your job is to keep quiet."

No doctor had ever shouted at Sister Josefina before, and she was shocked. In spite of her surprise, she snapped back, "I'm your responsible assistant. I'm going to tell you when you're making a mistake, whether you like it or not. And don't you shout at me like that again." After that, Dr. Walentowski always asked for Sister Josefina to assist him, though he continued to yell at her. He and his staff might do six or seven operations in a day. They spent all day in the operating room breathing ether, and sometimes they could become a little confused. Sister Josefina had to account for all the sponges and instruments and make sure that nothing was left inside a patient before the surgeon sewed him up.

Nuns like Sister Josefina played an important role in our rural life. Their presence and aid was a great comfort to the people in the villages.

If a person was dying, a nun would come to help right away, no matter how bad the weather or how far the journey. She would tend the patient and lead the family in prayer. Nuns traveled by bicycles in the summer. It was comical to see them cycling along wearing their big hats with their habits hitched up above their knees. In the winter, farmers transported them by sleigh. The nuns were devoted to our care and we all cherished them.

*   *   *

Health care was simpler in those days, and so were many other things, including communication. A hand-cranked telephone hung on the wall. When you turned the crank, the lady at the Post Office would answer, and then you would say, "Please connect me with such-and-such number," or the name of a business or farm. Other people with telephones could hear whatever you had to say. The Post Office had a telegraph machine, too. My sister Tina took me to see the operators sending out messages and the machine printing out telegrams, *tik-tik-tik*. We obtained most of our news from the newspaper. *Dziadzia* sent me down to the corner every morning to buy one. The newspaper was printed locally in Krobia, although most of the stories came over the telegraph. Radio was still new. When I was young, my uncles had a crystal radio with a little whisker for tuning. It was a challenge to use, and my uncles were always playing around with it. By the time the war came, we had a bigger radio, and we all listened to it in the evenings, until it was confiscated by the Nazis after the invasion.

Nowadays, people think they can't live the way we did, without indoor plumbing, modern communications, or electronic entertainment. Little do they know, everyone lived the same way not so very long ago, and some people still live without modern conveniences even in the U.S. I was more fortunate than many people, because I spent a healthy childhood on a well-run farm with the care and guidance of a loving family, especially *Dziadzia*.

5. Grabonog and Pudliszki

Dziadzia died from complications of diabetes in the winter of 1935, at the age of eighty-nine. After his death, my uncles Wlady and Stan ran the farm, and Ludwig helped out.

Mother's sister, Aunt Slawa, came from Berlin to attend *Dziadzia's* funeral. She told us at that time of the hardships being endured once again by people in Germany. Rationing was already in effect there because Hitler was preparing for war and supplies were dedicated to the military.

Slawa enjoyed the good meals we had on the farm and asked for help taking some food back to her family in Berlin without being arrested for black market trading. Her sisters told her they had a plan. Slawa was almost six feet tall and quite slender. She had worn a full-length coat of black sealskin on her train ride from Berlin. Zofia said, "Listen, Ludwig will butcher a pig and we'll make sausages. You're slim. You can just wrap the sausages around your waist, and I will ask Kasia to make some butter."

Slawa said, "I can carry the sausages around my waist, but I don't see how I can smuggle butter without it melting." Zofia sewed flat pockets all the way around the lower edges of the long coat so that it hung evenly. She and Kasia made butter, wrapped it in waxed paper, and froze it into flat packets. They wrapped the sausages around Slawa's waist, filled the pockets in the coat's hem with the butter packets, and Slawa rode the train back to Berlin. She told us later that it was a good thing the train was so cold, because no one could smell the sausages and the butter stayed frozen. The border inspector was very gallant and she had no trouble with him at all. He asked only for her papers and wished her a good journey. She said that when she got home she thought Uncle Hans would die, either from laughing as she unwrapped the sausages, or from anger at the risk she had taken.

*   *   *

When *Dziadzia* died, I was ten years old and my brother Wojciech was twenty. After leaving grammar school, Wojciech had found it hard to settle down to earn a living. He had thought he wanted to be a pharmacist, then a barber, and then a priest. He went to the famous seminary in Lublin, but he left after three years, complaining that it was a dirty nest of squabbles and backbiting, and not a place to lead a religious life. Mother did not like Wojciech talking about this in front me when I was a child, but when I was older he told me about the jealousy and bickering among the priests. After Wojciech left the seminary, he did his military service, and then he got a job as a bookkeeper on the Pudliszki estate.

Pudliszki was owned by the Pfanrich family. Despite their German-sounding name, they were Polish and had bought the estate from a German company after World War I. *Pani* Pfanrich was an old biddy who was eager to show off among the nobility, and her entire family acted like bigshots. In spite of their expensive habits, the Pfanrichs didn't like to pay for anything, including their taxes to the government. When Marshal Pilsudski, the premier of Poland, found that the Pfanrichs weren't paying their assessments, he sent tax inspectors. They found the thousands of acres of crops, the factory, the timber and sawmill — and no bookkeepers. Pilsudski installed a man named *Pan* Eugene to be the *treuhander*, or trustee, on the estate. *Pan* Eugene hired my brother Wojciech as a bookkeeper. The Pfanrich family was still allowed to live in the mansion, but they had to defer to the trustee. They reported their income to him, and they couldn't run up debt just because Madame Pfanrich wanted to act like a great lady.

*   *   *

After my sisters Tina and Maria finished Grade 7, our wealthy Aunt Cecylia paid the fees for them to attend a private secondary school on an estate called Poniec, about fifteen miles west of Krobia. The school was run by nuns and offered various vocational training programs for young women. The nuns ran the regional hospital there, as well as a villa for elderly ladies who could no longer care for themselves. Tina studied cooking and household management. Maria was not interested in home economics. She loved embroidery and lace making and hoped to earn a living selling her handiwork.

Tina was a good student. She found everything interesting and studied business and accounting along with cooking and sewing. She did very well. Maria's more adversarial approach to life led her to find conflict everywhere she went. Tina took advanced classes and worked in the smaller kitchen that prepared fine foods for the elderly ladies at the villa. Maria was offended that she didn't get to eat the fancy foods from the ladies' kitchen. She told the nun in charge of the main kitchen that the students' food was only fit for pigs and she wouldn't eat it. Tina said, "Maria, don't say that! Sister Katrina says you're insulting her, and you're making everything very difficult."

Maria replied, "Well, it's the truth! The food stinks!"

Tina said, "I eat that food and I'm healthy. It might not be the first-class meals that we got at home from Aunt Zofia, but it's good enough."

Maria said, "If we can't have the same food that the old ladies get, then I'm not eating it!" She was almost sent home, although she managed to finish her embroidery course.

Tina finished her secondary program with honors. As soon as she graduated, she was hired by a Krobia businessman, *Pan* Przywara. He was a German citizen who had lived in Poland since before World War I. He stayed in Krobia after independence because he had a good business buying grain from farmers and millers and exporting it to Germany. *Pan* Przywara was honest, he paid well, and he helped the poor. He even tried hiring drunks off the street to work in his granaries. The granaries were large rooms with open windows and good ventilation. Newly harvested grain needs to be turned frequently with rakes so that it dries properly. The drunks came and raked grain for a day. They got paid, went out and got drunk, and never came back. *Pan* Przywara said, "Well, I tried to help. Those bums just don't want to work."

Pan Przywara hired Tina to work in his office and considered her an excellent employee. She was good with bookkeeping and telephones, and like everyone else in our family, she spoke excellent German as well as Polish. She was also friendly and got along well with other people.

Tina worked for *Pan* Przywara for several years. Then Wojciech told her about an opening at the Pudliszki estate. The estate owners were members of fashionable society, and they frequently held banquets and entertained other stylish people. Tina told *Pan* Przywara, "I hate to leave you, but kitchen management is the profession that I trained for and I would like to work there." *Pan* Przywara said, "Krystina, please go with my blessing. I know those people, though. The first month that they don't pay you, you come back to me. This job will be waiting for you, because those people aren't reliable."

Pudliszki factory farm. The small structures are cold frames for cucumbers.

Wojciech was doing well at Pudliszki, saving his money and looking for a way to make our lives better. Within a year of *Dziadzia's* death, Wojciech found a place for us to rent in village called Grabonog, about twenty miles from Krobia. The village council had closed the school because there were no longer enough students to attend it, and they were looking for a tenant who would keep an eye on the property in exchange for nominal rent. There was space for a garden, so we could raise our own vegetables and we could keep a pig. I was happy with the move. I missed my Krobia friends, but there were new woods and fields to explore, and we settled in happily.

As soon as we moved to Grabonog, my mother bought a young pig from a local farmer. When it was grown, Uncle Ludwig came to our house to butcher it. He prepared the hams and sausages for smoking and then went back to Krobia. Before he left, Ludwig told Mother that our smokehouse had a problem and wasn't working right. Mother spoke to the *Burgermeister*, the city manager, who messed around with it a little, and said it was fixed. Mother started smoking the meat, but the fire

wouldn't stay lit. Mother called the *Burgermeister* back and told him it
was still broken. He insisted everything was fine. Mother tried to use the
smoker again, with no luck. She called the *Burgermeister* a third time and
persuaded him to go inside the smokehouse to take a look. Then she
locked him in. When I got home from school I could hear someone bang-
ing and hollering inside the smokehouse. I said, "Mother, there's someone in there! He'll get cooked!"

She said, "I know. Let him sit a little." When she let the *Burgermeister* out, he understood that he couldn't try to fool her just because she
was a woman on her own, and he fixed the smoker. Then we enjoyed
good sausages, smoked on apple chips.

When Maria finished at the Poniec school, she did some embroi-
dering and sold a few pieces, but she didn't make enough money to earn
a living, so she stayed with Mother and me in Grabonog. She never did
like cooking, but she helped around the house and worked in the garden.
There is always a lot of hand work on a farm, especially in the spring,
pulling weeds and hoeing to make the ground soft and airy, so Maria
made herself useful.

Mother, Maria, and I lived in Grabonog for several years, while I
finished grammar school nearby. I then planned to attend a vocational
institute to study forestry management and game keeping. In those days,
every estate employed a couple of forest managers who decided which
trees to cut for timber and firewood, how to keep the forest healthy, what
game animals to harvest, and how to keep nature in balance while using
its products. I loved spending my free time walking in the forest and I
hoped for a career working in the woods with wildlife and trees. However, this was not to be. Everyone's hopes and plans vanished and lives

were changed forever on September 1, 1939, when Poland was invaded by the Nazis.

PART II

1939 - 1945

6. The Invasion

In August of 1939, I was a gangly fourteen-year old schoolboy starting my last year of grammar school. All that summer, the radio had been broadcasting Hitler's speeches. He threatened invasion, internment, and death for every Pole. The Polish government responded with their own nationalist propaganda, inflaming anti-German prejudice. By late August, convoys of people from western Poland were passing through Grabonog as they fled the German border region. My uncles Stan and Wlady sent a telegram urging Mother, Maria, and me to hurry back to Krobia and join them as they led the rest of our family away from the border. Wojciech was already serving with the Polish army, preparing for the impending attack

When we got back to the farm, Mother asked my uncles, "What's the plan? Where will we go?"

Wlady said, "We have carts and horses ready. The invasion is about to start. We're heading east."

Mother replied, "But where can we go? To Russia? You know they hate us. They'll kill us when we get there."

Wlady said, "Well, anything looks better than staying here."

My third uncle, Ludwig, said, "I'm not running away with you. I think you're crazy! You're jumping right into the fire." He stayed behind on the farm, while the rest of my family—aunts, uncles, cousins, Mother, my two sisters, and I—all headed east with two carts and horses.

We travelled for two days and nights and had almost reached Warsaw when we saw the first German planes flying overhead. We stopped moving and camped with a crowd of other refugees at an estate called Gronowo. The estate's overseer allowed everyone to sleep in one of the sheep pastures. Some people slept in their carts and wagons. Maria and I were the youngest in our group, so we slept on piles of straw on the ground. We were so tired that we fell asleep as soon as we stopped moving. Once darkness fell, we awakened to squealing and yelling all around us. Rats were running up and down the carts and all over people. We stayed in the field that first night despite the rats, and I slept fine because I was so tired. When everyone started screaming again on the second night, Wlady said, "This is crazy!"

He went up to the estate's mansion and pounded on the door. He told the overseer, "You know the invasion has started. You have an obligation to give people shelter. You put everyone out in a bare field and you knew it was full of rats! No one can sleep out there! To keep the peace, you better let everyone in." The overseer listened to him, and that night we all slept inside the mansion on the floor of the ballroom.

The next day, the radio reported that German planes were attacking civilian convoys. My uncles feared a slaughter if we stayed out in the open. Wlady said, "To hell with it. Nothing can be worse than this. Let's go back to Krobia."

Wlady and Stan figured out how far the Germans had advanced in the four days since the start of the invasion. They calculated that if we left right away, and hurried, we'd get back to Krobia before the Germans reached our farm. We packed the cart and the uncles drove the horses back as fast as they could go. The German planes, the Stukas, were bombing and strafing along the roads. Whenever we saw planes, we ran away from the road and lay in ditches under the trees along the edges of the fields. The uncles made sure we avoided traveling with other groups, since the planes were targeting the crowds of refugees with machine gun fire and bombs. Carts and wagons were going east and west as people scrambled to find what they hoped was a refuge. Wlady and Stan were cautious, and they got us home safely.

My brother Wojciech's fiancée, Barbara, also fled to the east, together with her good friend Marina. Marina's husband was fighting with the Polish army against the Soviet forces on the eastern front. Marina had given birth to twin girls just three months before. The women and the babies were part of a crowd running along the road when they heard bombers coming. Everyone was screaming and yelling at one another to lie down in the ditches or run into the fields. Barbara held one baby, and Marina held the other. The bombs came down, and tore them apart. The two women were killed, but the babies lived. As Red Cross workers came and collected the bodies, they heard the babies crying. The baby girls were returned to their grandparents in Krobia. Barbara and Marina were buried in a mass grave with more than 300 other people, mostly women and children.

Marina's orphaned twins were raised by their grandparents. They were beautiful little blonde girls, and when they were three years old, the Nazis took them away to a special camp to be raised as Aryans. The grandparents almost lost their minds with grief. In spite of being taken away at such a young age, the girls somehow remembered their names and hometown during their separation. They were six years old when the war ended. The Red Cross helped the girls return to Krobia to be raised once again by their grandparents.

*   *   *

My family returned home without injury, although many civilians were killed during the German invasion. Then we waited to see what would happen to us.

We spent the day after we got home in a rush of activity — storing food for our family and fodder for the farm animals, hiding valuables, and praying. The radio reported that German soldiers were very close. Despite our preparations, none of us was ready for the heart-clutch that came when soldiers marched into our yard and pounded on the front door.

My sisters muffled their sobs as we stood behind the curtains in the upstairs front room. I peeked out into the farmyard and saw a crowd of German soldiers. Their uniforms and boots looked barely worn. Some of the men were holding the bridles of chestnut draft horses that were hitched to artillery. The horses were in excellent condition, glossy and well-fed, and their harnesses were high quality leather, thick and new. Polish radio reports of the invasion had said that the Germans were using worn-out nags harnessed with old ropes. I could see for myself that this was Polish government propaganda.

A German soldier hammered at the tall front door of our two-story farmhouse. Aunt Zofia opened it and said "*Guten tag.*" The soldier wore a sharply creased uniform and his boots were brightly polished. He looked Zofia up and down, said, "*Heil* Hitler," and strode into our entry hall. As he crossed the threshold, he slipped and fell sprawling across the polished floor. He yelled at Zofia, "You've set a trap! I fell! What's going on here? And why are you speaking German?"

Zofia replied, "I was born under Kaiser Wilhelm. I went to a German school. I've spoken German all my life. Everyone here speaks German."

The soldier said, "Shut up! This is clearly a trap!"

A German officer had followed the soldier inside, and now spoke sharply to him, "Silence! Are you crazy? These are cultured people. Their floors are clean and polished. You don't know how to walk in polite company." Thank goodness, the officer's response diverted the soldier's anger away from Zofia.

Zofia asked the officer, "How can we help you?"

The officer replied, "You will need to quarter four men here tonight. How many people live here now? Please show me around." Zofia described our family and showed him the two main rooms in the downstairs. She told him that she didn't have four beds. The officer replied, "Now that I've seen the inside of your house, we will place officers here rather than soldiers. They have their own cots, and your house will do very well for traveling quarters." Then four officers came in. They behaved very well. They were neat and quiet, and spoke to us politely.

That was our first contact with the German occupation forces. The next day they traveled on, but more German soldiers and officers came through every day, always taking quarters for the night and then moving on.

*   *   *

The German army entered Poland on September 1, 1939, and the Gestapo immediately began arresting people. In Krobia, they began by detaining some young Polish men who had offended a few of the ethnic German colonists living in the area by singing nationalist songs and yelling "Long live Poland!" Some of the colonists reported these boys to the Gestapo. The Gestapo also arrested local leaders, both civic and religious. One of the prisoners was a German doctor who was respected by Poles and Germans alike. The doctor owned an agricultural estate near my family's farm. He got in trouble when he asked the Gestapo not to arrest the chamberlain, who was an important Catholic official in our area and the Vatican representative for the Poznan district. The German doctor testified to the Gestapo that the chamberlain was not a Polish nationalist. The Gestapo arrested the chamberlain despite the doctor's intercession. They arrested the doctor too, even though he was German. The Gestapo locked their prisoners in the basement jail of the *Ratusz*, or City Hall. Every town had a *Ratusz*. It was traditionally built in the middle of the town's market square and had a jail in the basement where in normal times robbers or unruly drunks were kept until trial.

The Gestapo's prisoners were beaten and tortured until they were dazed and disoriented. The prisoners were forced to sign confessions to all kinds of crimes. A few weeks after the invasion, on October 21, 1939, the Gestapo posted placards all over Krobia announcing a mandatory public assembly. Everyone, including the German colonists, was ordered to gather in the market square. I went with my family, and we all stood together as the armed soldiers directed us. A German brass band played loud marches and military music from the back of an open truck. Soldiers with machine guns stood around the edges of the square. Then the Gestapo dragged six of the prisoners from the *Ratusz* jail out into the square. These were people we all knew, but they were so bloody and beaten we could barely recognize them. They trembled and staggered. Guards stood the prisoners against the wall of the *Ratusz* and ordered them to hold their hands up in the air. A line of six soldiers faced the prisoners. The command came. The soldiers shot. The prisoners fell on top of each other into a pile. Some were shot in the head or neck and died quickly. Some groaned and writhed for a long time. The soldiers brought up another six men and shot them, and then more, until there was a pile of dead and dying. The band played loud martial music from the back of their truck during the entire time, drowning out the cries of the crowd. One of the executed victims was my own cousin, Henryk Pawlicki. He was just a foolish teenager who had been reported to the Gestapo for singing patriotic songs.

After the shooting, the soldiers pulled some men and women out of the crowd at gunpoint and forced them to load the bodies into the back of a second truck. Some of the victims were still alive. I could hear them gargling and choking on their blood. The soldiers ordered everyone to march to the cemetery. The truck with the band—still playing at full volume—led the way, followed by the truck with the victims. The people who had loaded the truck walked next, followed by the rest of the townspeople.

The German doctor had been wounded but not killed. Some people dragged him off the truck on the way to the cemetery, and he survived. When we arrived at the cemetery, the soldiers forced people to unload the victims into a pit and shovel dirt into it. Some of the victims were still moving. Most of the German colonists in the crowd were horrified, but a few others—people whom my grandfather and uncles had thought were friends—cheered and clapped as they walked along.

I went straight home. I hadn't been there long, when Henryk's mother, my Aunt Basia, came into the hall. She knelt in front of the mirror in the hall and began to pray to Almighty God and the Blessed Mother. She was convinced that she was in church, praying in front of the Monstrance. She wasn't crying, but she couldn't hear me when I spoke to her. She just kept repeating the prayers. I called to my other aunts and told them that Basia had come from the executions and was in the hallway. They hurried out to her. Zofia said, "Oh, Basia, what are you doing here, my dear?" Basia began to recover her senses and her deranged prayers subsided into tears. My aunts took her into the kitchen and tried to soothe her. Late in the afternoon, Zofia said, "Come now. I will take you back to your house." They had to pass the *Ratusz* on their way, but they went around the square on the opposite side of the building so they wouldn't have to see the site of the murders.

The Gestapo committed similar atrocities in every town in our region. Their aim was to horrify so the populace wouldn't resist. A band always played loud martial music from the back of a truck during the executions so the crowd couldn't hear the prisoners' cries. The perversion of the musicians' talents and skills to the service of evil has always troubled me. Instead of bringing the beauty and inspiration that God intended, the music became the soundtrack to Nazi barbarity. I often wondered what those musicians were thinking as they were trucked from massacre to massacre.

*   *   *

As Hitler gained power in Germany before the war, many Jews who could afford to emigrate from Poland headed for Palestine. Having heard what was happening to the Jews in Germany, they believed Hitler's threats toward the Polish Jews. A few remained behind however, including *Pan* Zucker and my schoolmates, the Bilski boys.

Pan Grabowski was another Jew who stayed behind. He was a Jewish tanner and leatherworker who lived near us. His business was quite small, and he was not a rich man, but he worked hard and he treated everyone fairly. When we kids had a rabbit skin, we would take it to *Pan* Grabowski's shop, and he would pay us ten *groschen* for the skins. That was big money to us. *Pan* Grabowski sold the skins for twenty *groschen* after they were tanned, so he didn't make much for his work. When Uncle Ludwig warned him that the Germans were dangerous and advised him to emigrate, *Pan* Grabowski said, "Why would they bother me? I'm just a poor tradesman. Where could I go?"

Ludwig said, "Listen, Zigwisch, take your family and go to Palestine, because at least you'll be safe. In the eyes of the Nazis, you and your family are not citizens. You are not even human. You are only Jews."

Pan Grabowski and the other Jews who had stayed behind should have listened to Ludwig. Only a week after the German invasion, we awoke one morning to find that all of the Jewish families were gone. The Germans had come in the night and loaded them into the back of a truck. They were taken about forty miles away, into the woods south of Krotoszyn, and shot—men, women, and children, even the boys I knew from school. Ludwig said to us, "Didn't I tell you? I told *Pan* Grabowski to take his family and get out a long time ago. I knew Hitler would kill them. Hitler has been fueling hatred among the German people for a long time, first hatred for the Jews and then for the Poles. Hitler told the people that he would get rid of the millionaires. He's dealing with them in secret while he's killing the poor people, Jews and Poles."

7. The Occupation's Early Days

After the German invasion, in September of 1939, Mother, Maria, and I did not return to Grabonog, but moved back to the farm in Krobia with Tina and our aunts and uncles. Wojciech had not been captured in the few days of action that he saw and he also returned to the farm soon after the invasion. When he got home, he was so covered with lice that Mother had to burn his clothes and shave his entire body.

I was supposed to attend one more year of grammar school, but the Nazis limited Polish kids to only four years of schooling. All the Polish teachers disappeared. The only teacher who stayed was *Herr* Flans, a German who had come to Krobia during Kaiser Wilhelm's rule and stayed on after Polish independence in 1918. He was joined by two sisters, the *Frauleinen* Schultz, who had taught in Krobia before independence. Afterwards, they went to Breslau to teach, but when the Germans came back in 1939, the two women returned to Krobia.

Once the Nazis were in charge, German students attended a separate school. I had already passed through Grade 6, but Mother knew *Fraulein* Schultz, and she agreed to let me stay on for part of one more year. After the invasion, although we spoke Polish at home, the Polish students were required to read, write, and speak only German at school. The Nazis wanted Polish workers to understand their orders.

Before the invasion, I had been good friends with a boy named Bubi Gross. He was the son of a German colonist who lived near our farm. Bubi and I were schoolmates and we ran around together in the summers. After the invasion, Poles were ordered to step into the gutter if we met a German walking on the sidewalk. We had to take off our caps, bow, and say "Good day." I will never forget the day I saw Bubi walking towards me with a couple of other boys. I ran up to him and said, "Bubi, how are you? I haven't seen you in quite a while." He hauled off and slugged me so hard in the mouth that I was knocked down into the street.

He said, "Stay there! That's where you belong. From now on, I am *Herr* Gross. We are not friends. I don't even know you."

I said, "What are you talking about? Did I say something wrong? Forgive me!" Bubi just kept walking.

I tried to avoid him after that incident, which was easy because he soon joined the army, even though he was only sixteen. I met his sister in the summer of 1941. She greeted me in tears and said, "Andreas, my mother still can't forget how Bubi treated you. We are so sorry. I don't know if you've heard—Bubi is dead now."

I said, "What on earth happened?" She told me that he'd been killed on the Russian front a week after he'd been sent there.

After I told Mother of Bubi's death, she went to give her condolences to his mother. *Frau* Gross said, "*Pani* Jurkowska, I wish all of the Poles and Germans were like you people. Then we wouldn't have any wars." *Frau* Gross remained friends with my mother, but Bubi was her only son, and she never recovered from his death.

*   *   *

Soon after the massacre in Krobia, the Gestapo closed almost all the churches and began removing the Catholic priests from our area. Most of the priests from the nearby Chumientki estate disappeared, and we learned that they had been taken to concentration camps. Mother rescued two priests by hiding them in our farmhouse basement. The house had a main cellar with a door that opened to the outside. There was also a separate, smaller cellar under the kitchen that was accessed through a trap door hidden under the linoleum floor covering. The two priests, Doctors Karol Brzezina and Meinkowski, hid in that small space for several weeks. Mother kept their presence a secret from everyone in the family, since the penalty for concealing wanted individuals was death. Mother brought food and water to the priests at night, and emptied the bucket they used as a chamber pot. The priests received just a small amount of light and ventilation from a tiny window high up in one wall. Mother arranged to get them passports from an official she knew in Krobia, and the priests eventually escaped to Italy by train. Father Meinkowski served with Polish troops under British command in Italy. Father Brzezina served with British troops in India. They continued corresponding with Mother until their deaths many years later.

*   *   *

As soon as the Germans had conquered Poland, they seized control of agricultural and industrial production and put SS overseers in charge of the estates. SS stood for the *Schutzstaffel*, the Nazi paramilitary organization responsible for general policing in the occupied territories. Werner Stöver was the SS officer assigned to Pudliszki, the estate where Wojciech and Tina worked before the invasion.

Herr Stöver was from an old German military family. He had grown up in Berlin and had an SS tattoo. He had some familiarity with Poland because he had visited several times before the war. A champion sprinter and hurdler for Germany during the 1930's, he won a medal at the European Championships held in Warsaw the year before the Berlin Olympics.

The Polish owners of Pudliszki, the Pfanrichs, fled when the war started. Once the fighting stopped, they tried return to Pudliszki. Stöver told the Pfanrichs to talk to the occupation government in Warsaw. The Nazis sent them to a special occupation zone called the General Government, which had been set up in eastern Poland for wealthy and upper class Poles. We never saw the Pfanrichs again.

After Stöver took over Pudliszki, he interviewed all the people who had been working in the estate offices. Everyone who spoke German was sent back to their jobs. Wojciech returned to bookkeeping and eventually worked his way up to the position of chief bookkeeper for the entire estate. Although he never had formal training, Wojciech was smart and hard-working. The fact that he spoke excellent German, thanks to our grandfather's encouragement, also helped his advancement.

Tina (first row, second from left) with Pudliszki staff

Tina was also well-placed. When the Germans invaded, Tina had left her job managing the Pudliszki mansion for the Pfanrichs and moved back to our farm. After Stöver brought his wife, Charlotte, from Berlin, *Frau* Stöver asked who had been the estate's domestic manager, and she was told about Tina. At the same time, Tina's former boss from the grain business, *Pan* Przywara, sent a letter recommending her to the Stövers. They were pleased to get a reference from a German citizen, and called Tina for an interview. She spoke excellent German and was clearly qualified, so Stöver rehired her to be the mansion's manager.

*   *   *

Since I was now fourteen, I could no longer attend school. I had to get a job and so did my sister Maria, who was then in her early twenties. We were worried that if we didn't find work quickly, the Germans would send us to a labor camp. Uncle Ludwig said to Maria and me, "See what has happened to our country? They will never get out. Never! You'd better polish up your German in a hurry because you will be working under them. There is no way out of this for us." Fortunately, Stöver already had a good opinion of Wojciech and Tina, so he hired Maria and me as well.

Maria was put to work in the estate gardens that grew vegetables for the exclusive German market. The market had controlled prices and only German people in the area were permitted to shop there—no Poles were allowed. The estate gardens also grew produce for the German administrators who lived in the mansion. Maria enjoyed working there and developed into a skillful gardener, but in her heart, she retained the love for sewing and fashion that she inherited from Father and Mother.

I began by working in the canning factory on the estate. Stöver and the other Germans called me Andreas, the German version of Andrzej. Stöver soon promoted me to be an assistant in the factory office. He liked me because in addition to speaking good German. I was tall, slim, and in good physical shape, and as a sports enthusiast and follower of Nazi doctrine on health and physical culture, Stöver valued athleticism. He frequently belittled the heavy German colonists.

Poles were not allowed to possess bicycles during the war, but Stöver got me a special permit, and I went to work as the main delivery boy for the estate. Every day the office sent packages and papers around the estate, from the mansion to the factory office, and from the estate to the post office in Krobia. I rode with bulky packages tied on either side of my bicycle and another hanging on the rear. During the summer, the job wasn't too bad, but the snow was merciless in the winter. All six winters of the war were extremely harsh. The snow sometimes came up to my knees and I cried many times. I had to push the bicycle instead of riding it and it was cold as all hell. I was frequently late finishing my route, which was very stressful, since the police enforced a strict curfew on all Poles, and I would have been beaten and jailed if they had met me on the road after curfew. Eventually I asked for permission to start my route an hour earlier. Stöver asked me why and I told him the snow was so deep that I couldn't pedal the bicycle, but had to walk the whole way pushing it with the packages hanging down. Stöver laughed and called me a silly little plum. Then he gave me permission to start my route whenever I wanted.

*   *   *

The *Gauleiter* (Governor) of the Poznan region was Arthur Greiser. He became infamous as the organizer and head of the Holocaust in our part of Poland. After the war, he was convicted for crimes against humanity at the Nuremburg trials and hanged for his acts.

Early in Stöver's administration of Pudliszki, *Gauleiter* Greiser assigned an SA man, *Herr* Hause, to assist Stöver, and also to spy on him. The SA, or *Sturmabteilung* (Storm Detachment), was the original paramilitary wing of the Nazi party. The SS, or *Schutzstaffel* (Protection Squadron) had been a branch of the SA before it was separated in a series of reorganizations in the early 1920s. There was tremendous distrust and suspicion between the rival services.

The ongoing rivalry between the SS and the SA led to antagonism between Stöver and Hause. Stöver resented having the *Gauleiter's* agent observing him. Hause was worried about a purge of SA officers, so he tried to oust Stöver by maligning him to the *Gauleiter*. Stöver's own spies told him about Hause's treachery, so Stöver went to the *Gauleiter* to defend his management of Pudliszki. In the end, the *Gauleiter* sided with Stöver. He kept Hause in Poznan, while Stöver continued to run the Pudliszki estate. Stöver finally convinced the *Gauleiter* that Hause was untrustworthy and the *Gauleiter* transferred Hause to the eastern front.

Stöver looked after his own skin by running the factory and farm efficiently and meeting his production goals. He also bribed as many high-ranking officials as he could. Corruption within the Nazi organization ran deep. Hitler would have executed all his officers if he had known about their bribe-taking, corruption, and black market dealing. Stöver held lavish banquets at the mansion and invited Nazi officials from all over western Poland, including *Gauleiter* Greiser and even the Governor-General of Poland, Hans Frank. Frank had been Hitler's personal lawyer, and he became the chief jurist in occupied Poland. Frank oversaw the exclusion and murder of millions of Jews and others and he was executed after the war.

*   *   *

My sister Maria and several of her girlfriends were required to serve as waitresses at Stöver's banquets. On one occasion, they decided to demonstrate their resistance to the Nazi regime by wearing red skirts and white blouses—the colors of the Polish flag. The Nazis were outraged and the next day the girls were hauled in to the police station and beaten, so they never tried that trick again. They were lucky—others were sent to Auschwitz for similar offenses. Auschwitz was well known and everyone understood that it was a death camp. I never believe it when I hear people claim they had no idea about what was going on there. The Nazis controlled Poland through terror and murder right from the start, and everyone was aware of it.

The Pudliszki farm and factory supplied the German war effort on the Russian front. Stöver also provided the army with cannon fodder. Many German bureaucrats wanted to work at Pudliszki, since it was viewed as a relatively safe haven from the war. Stöver welcomed all comers. However, the minute *Gauleiter* Greiser said, "Stöver, I need reinforcements," Stöver would transfer his new assistants into the active military.

Stöver put a lot of effort into insulating himself from being sent to the front. He bribed his cronies all over Germany and Poland with a constant flow of the estate's best goods, sending regular gifts of extra-special jams and preserves to Gestapo officers in Berlin and to the *Gauleiter* in Poznan so they wouldn't transfer him. Stöver also sent delicacies to his family in Berlin. He kept a locked storage room with boxes of the finest goods stacked higher than his head. Sometimes a Gestapo truck would come from Berlin to be loaded with goodies. Other Germans around the estate noticed this and grumbled about it. When they asked Stöver for special products, he would ask where their ration cards were. They didn't like this, but if they complained, he sent the men off to the front and transferred their families to other estates. They didn't come back. Stöver was the dictator of his own little empire, and he didn't want any opposition from his German brethren. So much for the Brotherhood of the Aryan Nation that the Nazis were always preaching.

Wilhelm Krüger, the chief Gestapo commander of Poland, visited Stöver once. He brought his own truck to be loaded with delicacies. Stöver called me in to meet him, saying, "Andreas, this is Commander Krüger. Go and pack. He's come to take you to Auschwitz."

I turned pale and said, "*Jawohl*, Herr Stöver."

They both laughed and Stöver said, "Oh, Andreas, I was only joking." Big joke, hah.

Another time, an important Gestapo official came to collect his payoff. He was a member of the old German nobility and Stöver treated him with great deference. Stöver's pride in bribing a prince of the old regime belied his lip service to the ideal of Nazi brotherhood.

The authorities in Berlin transferred a German agronomist named Fischer to Pudliszki to help increase the estate's output. Fischer and his wife set up a scheme for trading from the estate's chicken flock on the side, selling eggs and chickens on the black market. When Stöver discovered their tricks, Fischer was sent to the Russian front. Stöver managed to get almost all the Germans who were sent to assist him transferred. He was in cahoots with *Gauleiter* Greiser in Poznan and an SS bigshot in Berlin, and he easily convinced them that his German assistants would be more useful doing actual fighting. One who especially remains in my memory was a man named Dietrich. He was a classic Aryan specimen, the perfect stud for making Hitler's children— blond and arrogant as hell. He got too cocky with Stöver, and he, too, was dispatched to the eastern front never to return. Stöver was fortunate, because not one of the men he sent away ever came back. He himself would say, "Have you heard? Dietrich is dead, Fischer is dead." Stöver's SA rival, Hause, survived, however. I saw him myself after the war when I was traveling on an express train in West Germany.

8. Life Under the Germans

Poles and Germans alike quickly learned to keep their mouths shut and their opinions to themselves. Many Germans believed Hitler when he told them that their first loyalty was to the Reich, not to their families, and that they had an obligation to report anyone, even their own parents, for anti-Nazi sympathies.

My mother's sister Slawa and her German husband Hans continued to live with their sons in Berlin. Rationing had been tough since the mid-1930s, and it tightened further after the war began. Everything was dedicated to building and then supporting the military. In her letters to us, Slawa told of food shortages. Ludwig felt sorry for his sister, so he butchered a pig in secret. He planned to prepare sausages and hams to smuggle into Berlin, as he and his Krobia sisters had done before, in direct violation of the German regulations against smuggling food. Ludwig was betrayed by my cousin Zosia, Uncle Max's daughter. Zosia was outraged and jealous that Ludwig was sending good sausages to Berlin. Without asking if she could have some sausages for herself, she informed the Gestapo. The military police came while Ludwig and Zosia's brother Stefan were in the middle of butchering. Both men were arrested and sent to Wronki Prison.

Wronki was about a hundred miles away, northwest of Poznan, and the harshest prison in Poland. A month or two after the arrest, a man who had been released from the prison came to tell my aunts what had happened to Ludwig. He had been beaten so terribly that his kidneys failed and he died. The man said he couldn't understand why the guards had beaten Ludwig to death. When the Germans spoke to him, he had answered them in perfect German. My cousin Stefan survived. The Germans put him to work building a road through a swamp during freezing winter weather, but he was a strong young man and lived through the ordeal.

Hans and Slawa, in Berlin, were devastated at the news of Ludwig's death. They couldn't believe that Zosia would betray her uncle and brother over sausages. But Slawa was also naïve about the political situation. A woman who lived downstairs from their Berlin apartment was known to be an ardent supporter of Hitler's policies. Without thinking, Slawa divulged her feelings about the *Führer*. The woman informed the Gestapo and they came to interrogate Slawa. She was able to talk her way out of being arrested. Slawa later said, "I couldn't believe that woman would denounce me because I spoke my mind to her. We've known each other for many years. I knew she was a gossip—but I thought I could trust her."

Before the war, many middle-class, educated Berliners considered Jews to have been completely assimilated into modern German life. Slawa and Hans's sons, Siegfried and Raimond were no different. They each had many Jewish and atheist friends and they studied under Jewish professors at the University of Berlin. As the anti-Jewish Nuremburg laws began to take effect in Berlin and elsewhere in the mid 1930s, Siegfried and Raimond became active participants in anti-Nazi demonstrations. Hans warned them to be careful because the level of anti-Jewish violence was increasing. One evening, Siegfried and Raimond attended a large demonstration against Nazi policies. The protesters were surrounded by SA troops, stripped naked, and beaten with batons until they were bloody and reeling. After the beatings ended, the SA told them to go on home naked. Siegfried staggered into a shop and telephoned his parents. Slawa and Hans brought clothes and helped the boys home. Slawa said afterwards that her boys were so bruised and bloody that the only parts of them she could recognize were their butts.

*   *   *

Stöver had no respect for the *Volksdeutsch*, the ethnic German colonists who had settled in western Poland and were living in our area when the Nazis arrived. I often heard Stöver say that the *Volksdeutsch* were nothing but fat lumps who didn't want to work. He said they were loafers who only wanted to give orders to the Poles and eat fine foods. Stöver preferred having Poles around him, because he knew he had the power of the Gestapo to enforce his dictates.

One of the *Volksdeutsch* colonists who had continued farming in Poland after independence was *Herr* Neugebauer. Stöver might have dismissed him as a big, fat man with a big, fat family, but *Herr* Neugebauer was anything but lazy. He was a hard-working farmer and managed his estate so that it was very prosperous. The Neugebauer family had always gotten along well with the Poles and never had a bad word for anyone. I went to school with some of the Neugebauer boys, and thought of them as my friends. After the Germans conquered Poland and were besieging cities in Russia, *Herr* Neugebauer told Uncle Wlady, "Listen, the tree that loses its blossoms and leaves in the spring will never bear fruit in the summer." He was implying that Hitler was paying too high a price for his advances in the east and that Germany could never win the war.

More Germans continued to move in around us. A year or two after the invasion, the German authorities opened western Poland to resettlement by Germans who had been displaced by the war. Stöver personally disapproved of this policy. Settling more Germans in his jurisdiction increased the risk that he might lose his authority and be sent to the front.

When the Krobia area opened to German resettlement, *Frau* Meyer came to town. She was from the Sudetenland, in Czechoslovakia, and her husband was an officer serving on the Russian front. After looking around the area, she chose our farm for her new home. She and her children lived in the downstairs rooms, obliging my aunts and uncle to move upstairs, where I lived with Mother, Tina, and Maria, making seven of us in all. *Frau* Meyer employed my uncles to run the farm as they had done before the war, while my aunts cooked and cleaned for her. She was unhappy because she was required to provide a set amount of grain and cattle to the military. *Frau* Meyer didn't like either the work or the expense, so she sold off most of the livestock and pocketed the money. Eventually a government agent came to ask why her contributions were getting smaller and smaller. She told him that the crops were bad and she couldn't afford to feed the livestock, but we knew she had bribed the agent to keep quiet.

Aunt Cecylia, the eldest of my aunts and uncles, had been married to a German man, entitling her to *Reichsdeutsch* citizenship, and as a widow she owned her manor in Pomerania outright. Nevertheless, she was evicted in favor of a German family and was obliged to move back to the farm in Krobia with her brothers and sisters. This was a fortunate turn of events because the extra rations she received as a *Reichsdeutsch* citizen helped support the family.

*   *   *

A hamlet called Kokoszki stood at the gates of the Pudliszki factory. When the war started, Polish workmen constructed barracks there for the factory and farm workers, and Wojciech shared an apartment with some of the other bookkeepers. We were all happy when Stöver made another Kokoszki apartment available for my family after *Frau* Meyer and her family moved into the ground floor of our farmhouse. Mother, Tina, Maria, and I moved to Kokoszki for the duration of the war. Each family in the barracks was allotted a garden plot. The location was convenient and it was less crowded than in our farmhouse.

Our flat had three rooms — a small kitchen, the main room, which was a combined dining room and living room, and a bedroom. In winter, we usually ate in the kitchen because it was warmer. We kept the door to the living-dining room closed, but we allowed the warmth from the kitchen to flow into the bedroom. Friends often came over in the evenings and we played cards and told stories. Occasionally Wojciech held an evening meeting with some of his buddies. He would give me a look that let me know I had to leave while they talked. I wasn't sure what they discussed, but I'm sure it was related to resistance activities.

Evening gathering in our Kokoszki flat (clockwise from left: Wojciech, Jurek,
Maria, Andrzej, Tina, cousin Jolanta, Waleria, Jurek's sister Marina

I had been working for Stöver as the Pudliszki delivery boy for a few months when a huge furor erupted and I was called to the main office. A check for 60,000 marks from the factory to one of our suppliers had disappeared. The police wanted to question me because I had carried the envelope containing the check from the factory to the post office in Krobia. I waited in the corridor outside one of the mansion's ballrooms while the military police interrogated the three Polish bookkeepers, including my brother Wojciech and an older man, *Pan* Zigmund. I could hear the police screaming and shouting at the men, along with the sounds of kicking and punching. Old *Pan* Zigmund was obviously confused by the shouting and beating because he started to say things about the bookkeeping process that I knew to be wrong. I knocked until one of the policemen came to the door and said, "What do you want?"

I said, "*Pan* Zigmund is giving you wrong answers because he's confused and nervous."

The policeman said, "I'll show you nervous," and he slapped me across the face.

I was shocked, but I kept my temper and said only, "Excuse me. I was trying to help."

The policeman replied, "We don't need help, you idiot. We're taking care of it." Then he slammed the door. After another ten minutes, they dragged the three bookkeepers out—all black and blue. Then they took me into the enormous room. They smacked me around a little, but I wasn't treated too badly, because all they could ask me was what I had done with the letter when I took it to the post office. Of course, the post office always issued a signed receipt for letters like that, and the receipt was right there in the file.

Stöver asked me if the police had beaten me, so I told him what happened. He said, "Andreas, you should never open your mouth when they are shouting and beating."

I said, "But *Herr* Stöver, it hurt me when I knew they were beating *Pan* Zigmund until he was confused and started saying things that weren't true."

Pan Zigmund sat in jail for several weeks, but the check remained missing.

At that time, Stöver's first assistant for the factory's financial activities was *Herr* Korzanowski, a Polish man who was married to a *Reichsdeutsch* woman. When Germany took over, Korzanowski was reclassified as *Volksdeutsch* instead of Polish so he could work in a position of responsibility. The Korzanowskis had a beautiful daughter who fell in love with a *Leutnant zur See*, a lieutenant in the German Navy. The wife and daughter wanted an extravagant wedding, and *Herr* Korzanowski wanted to make them happy and look like a big shot among all the Germans.

In discussing the missing money with Stöver, my brother Wojciech suggested that he might want to investigate how Korzanowski was planning to pay for his daughter's fancy wedding. Stöver jumped on Wojciech's hint. He had Korzanowski arrested and brought to the office, where he confessed to the theft right away. Korzanowski had cashed the check and let the Polish bookkeepers take the blame. Stöver was furious and shouted at Korzanowski like a wild animal. He said, "What happened here? You swine! I should kick you right in the mouth so that you can never talk again. You knew those men were being beaten by the police and the boy Andreas was questioned, and you sat there and did nothing!" He threw Korzanowski to the police and they took him away.

Stöver told me he knew I could have had nothing to do with it, because a kid like me wouldn't know what to do with all that money.

After Korzanowski's arrest, Wojciech was given a lot more responsibility. He was put in charge of checking back through all the old accounts to see if money had been stolen in the past. He did a good job and was promoted to head bookkeeper.

I was also given a promotion. I had been the mail boy for about eighteen months when the Korzanowski incident occurred. Not long afterwards, Stöver told me to start working in the office full time. He didn't trust the German man who was operating the telephone exchange. Stöver said to me, "Andreas, I'm going to give you a new job. You speak good German. I want you to operate the central telephone exchange, since the man who's there now is leaving for the eastern front. I'll tell you what to do and what to say."

My sister Maria spoke good German too, but she stuck to Polish. She got into trouble when Stöver asked her why I spoke such good German while she didn't. In perfect German, she replied, "I will not speak German until Hitler wins this war, and he hasn't won it yet." Stöver slapped her mouth and then beat her across her back and shoulders with his stick for her insolence.

I began my new job as the main switchboard operator in the late summer of 1941. Whenever the phone rang, I would answer in German, and put the call through by moving the cord on the plug to the correct outlet. I would then hang up so I didn't overhear the conversation.

When I started working in the estate's office, a few Germans were still employed there, although most of the men were eventually drafted into the army and most of the women returned to Germany. One of the nicest women was *Fraulein* Gross, the daughter of a high official in Berlin who served as Stöver's private secretary. She and her good friend *Fraulein* Tomas were both working at the office when I started there. *Fraulein* Tomas was obviously Jewish and I couldn't understand how she had survived so long. In July of 1941, *Fraulein* Tomas was arrested and taken to Auschwitz, where she was finished off. *Fraulein* Gross was very depressed by this and returned to her family in Berlin soon after.

Frau Stöver carried a little silver revolver that she happily showed off to everyone around her. She told us she carried it because she had been warned to be afraid of the Poles. However, Stöver and his wife chose to surround themselves with Poles rather than Germans. For example, *Frau* Stöver asked for Polish Catholic nuns to attend her when she went to the Poniec hospital for the birth of her son, Jürgen. This was on the same estate where Tina and Maria had studied and was the closest hospital to Pudliszki. The staff included German nurses, as well as some of the Polish Catholic nursing sisters who had remained after the hospital was taken over by the Germans. Dr. Walentowski was also still working there. Stöver liked him, even though the Walentowski family was Catholic, and many Nazis were anti-Catholic.

When the baby was due, Stöver went to the hospital and told the Director, "My wife will be coming here. She is being examined by Dr. Walentowski right now, and the baby will arrive soon. I want her attended only by the Polish Catholic sisters that she asks for."

The Director said, "We don't allow you to make that choice here."

Stöver said, "Listen carefully to what I am saying. I am an SS officer. I want only Polish Catholic nursing sisters to care for my wife." The Director looked back at him, and obeyed his order.

I heard this story from Sister Louisa, the nun who stood at the hospital gate to admit people. Once Stöver revealed he was an SS officer, he got what he wanted. Only the Catholic sisters cared for his baby and his wife. When the Stövers left the hospital, one Catholic sister carried the baby to the Mercedes and the other Catholic sisters helped *Frau* Stöver to the car while the German nurses remained inside.

*   *   *

One morning in the spring of 1942, when I had just turned seventeen, I was so sick that I couldn't get out of bed. My brother Wojciech went to Stöver and said, "*Herr* Stöver, I have a big favor to ask. Andreas is very sick. He's vomiting, he has a high fever, and a huge pain in his belly." Stöver said, "Take him to the Poniec hospital right away. I will tell my driver Zigmund to use my Mercedes. You go home, prepare your brother, and Zigmund will take him there."

I don't remember much of the trip because I was in a lot of pain. My appendix had ruptured and the infection had spread. When we arrived at the hospital, I was relieved to hear that my surgeon would be Dr. Walentowski. He operated right away and he and his team worked on me for more than four hours. My friend, Sister Josefina, told me later that the assistant surgeon was forced to leave the operating room because the stench was so terrible. She told me, "You are very lucky to be alive, because the infection was everywhere. You have no idea how many cloths we had to use to clean it out."

Stöver himself came to visit me in the hospital the next day. This was very decent of him — in fact, I couldn't quite believe it. I heard him teasing and joking with Sister Louisa in the hallway, and then he came into my room. He saw how miserable I was and I have never forgotten how he gave me a little tap on the cheek, and said, "Andreas, get healthy, because I need you back working in the office. When they let you out of the hospital, you rest for two weeks at your flat, and then you come back to work. I have already talked to Dr. Walentowski. He tells me that two weeks of recuperation at home will be enough. Then you can start walking and working again."

Stöver showed some humanity then, and not only with me. He took care of the estate's other workers when they were sick. He employed a German nurse to give him health reports every week about who was sick and what the doctor said about their recovery times. He listened to the doctor's recommendations and allowed people time off in order to prevent general outbreaks of illness. Of course, his motivation was to keep the estate's workforce strong enough to meet production goals, so he wouldn't be transferred to active military service as punishment for failure.

*   *   *

Under the German regime, the local people who worked in the fields were given a share of the crops and some money every month. The people in the offices and factories got paid weekly. The wages were lower than they had been before the war, and we had to pay taxes for the military, but we didn't complain out loud because we all knew how lucky we were to be working at Pudliszki. Life was a lot worse in most other places in Poland and beyond.

The German administration issued every family *Lebensmittel Karten* — ration books, with stamps distributed monthly for foods and other goods. We were told to be thankful that Adolf was thinking about us. Everything was rationed — food, clothing, shoes, and fuel for cooking and heating. The food allocations were the bare minimum for survival, so people contrived ways to get along. Each family was allotted specific quantities of various foods per week. The German citizens also had ration books, although their allowances were larger.

During the occupation, everyone heated and cooked with wood stoves and Stöver saw to it that every family got firewood. The estate harvested and milled timber, so scraps and diseased wood were rationed and distributed for heating. Everywhere we went, we picked up twigs and branches dropped by trees along the roadsides and ditches and carried them home for kindling. Everyone also had a special *Besuchsschein*, a permit, for coal. My sister Tina's former employer, the merchant *Pan* Przywara, sold coal in addition to grain. Once a month we pulled a little sledge the two or three miles from our apartment in Kokoszki to his store in Krobia to buy our ration.

*   *   *

Our rations allotted us pound of flour per month and one egg per week per person. Each family received a pound of margarine, a pound of sugar, and a pound of lard per month. The authorities kept track of everything people grew for themselves. If you had your own hens and grew grain to feed them, an inspector would order some of the eggs and grain taken to be sold, and you wouldn't be issued any ration stamps for eggs. If you had a cow, you had to give the milk and butter to the government inspector. Naturally, the farmers skimmed off some of the cream and added water to what was left so they could have a little butter. There was always some kind of double-dealing going on.

Groceries sold to Poles were inferior, and we were only allowed to shop on Fridays. The shopkeepers called Friday "Pig's Day" because many Germans had taken to calling us pigs or worse since the occupation began, even though we had all lived amicably together before the war. Polish Catholics observed Fridays as meatless fast days, and some of the shopkeepers sold Poles meat that was already turning bad, since they knew we wouldn't be eating the meat for another day. We could buy only ribs or leg bones with very little meat on them and the quality grew worse as the war went on. In the early days, the bakery began to mix sawdust into the bread. By the end of the war, a loaf was more than half sawdust and wood chips.

Each fall during the German occupation, after the crops had been harvested, Stöver gave us permission to go into the fields and gather a few kilos of leftover grain or potatoes. He said, "If the police stop you, tell them you have permission from me. But I can't save you if you exceed the amount I've approved for you, and remember, I depend on you to be here in the office every day." Maria and I went out and picked up as much grain as we were allowed. We paid a man who lived near us for the use of his illicit hand mill. The mill had two grindstones, with a stick set into the side of the top one. We poured the grain into a hole in the middle and took turns pushing the stick on the side to rotate the upper stone over the lower one. The coarse grounds ran out into a bucket set underneath. Nobody ever informed on the man, even though some people were envious that he made extra money with his grindstone.

Stöver assigned each family a garden plot. We grew two rows of potatoes, which were a great help in supplementing our rations. We also had carrots, cabbage, kohlrabi, cucumbers, and dill for our pickles, and we grew spinach for harvest in the fall. That little garden fed us throughout the war years. After a day at work I was tired, but I didn't sit around and wait for dinner to appear. As soon as I got home, I pulled weeds and pumped water for the vegetable garden. To store food for winter, I dug a pit about three feet across. I put straw in the bottom, and we packed the pit with cabbages, carrots, and rutabagas—our vegetables that kept well. We wrapped them in straw, put them in the pit, and covered the top of the pile with straw and leaves. I piled dirt on top until the mound was about two feet high. When Mother needed something to cook, I used a pick to break the ground open. Because I had packed the pit in an organized way, I knew which side to open. I would reach in and pull out a cabbage or some carrots, and then pack everything back up. Maria was too squeamish to reach into the dirt and straw because a mouse once ran up her arm. She said she would rather go hungry than have that happen again.

*   *   *

I was permitted to keep a pair of rabbits. Mother and Maria spun the fur into yarn using a drop spindle after the Germans confiscated our spinning wheel. This was much slower than spinning with a wheel, so I would help by turning the spindle for them. The rabbits bred well, so we ate rabbit a couple of times a month. Their favorite food was dandelions, so I dug up a few wherever I went. In the summer, I walked along the ditches and cut grass with a sickle. I brought it home rolled up in a cloth and dried it to make hay for the rabbits' bedding and for them to eat in the winter. Our rutabagas were also good for the rabbits. I would take one out, cut it up with the leaf and the stalk, and let the pieces freeze so the rabbits could gnaw on it. Their teeth were always growing, so it was important for them to have something hard to chew on. In the spring, we tilled any leftover vegetables back into the garden.

Because the authorities knew we had rabbits, my family did not receive the regular meat ration. We were allotted a kilo of sausage per month because the authorities knew we couldn't make sausages out of rabbit. Having rabbits and sausage was better than having meat coupons and shopping at the butcher, where the meat was nothing but scraped bones and gristle.

After Mother traded a couple of our hens for a rooster, the hens laid fertile eggs. We raised the chicks until they were big enough to eat, then slaughtered them. Mother cooked the meat and canned it in jars with her pressure cooker. We were supposed to turn the eggs over to the inspector, but Mother always managed to set a few aside, and she was shrewd at bartering eggs for other supplies.

We were always happy to get our lard ration. Mother made it into something delicious. First she melted a little lard and used it to fry a panful of chopped onions until they were soft and golden. Then she melted and added the rest of the lard. The mixture kept well and the onion flavor made the lard more palatable. Mother dipped our bread straight into the melted fat. When we ate it, we tasted the onion flavor, and couldn't tell that it was only lard. It satisfied us.

Many people ate duck but preferred beef or pork lard to duck fat. Mother knew a store that sold ducks, so she agreed to trade eggs for any extra duck fat. We ate the duck fat on bread, Mother cooked sauces with it and even mixed it with potatoes to make potato salad without mayonnaise. Somehow it never seemed to spoil. For other meals, Mother added finely chopped vegetables to the gravy and mixed it up with potatoes. It was surprisingly good.

Late in the fall, Mother would wash the spinach and put it in bags made of *pargamana*, which is something like waxed paper. We kept the spinach frozen all through the winter. Mother would defrost it, fry it with a little onion and lard, and serve it over mashed potatoes. She would always say, "Just imagine you have meat." We were always hungry, but the onions made everything smell good. We longed for bacon, but there was none to be had. Of course, any leftovers went into soup. Mother often said, "Today it's potatoes with soup, and tomorrow it's soup with potatoes."

We had fruit in the summer. Early in the war, Stöver let people buy whatever was plentiful at harvest time. Everyone was quick to make jam or marmalade although this was difficult, since there wasn't enough sugar to make good jam. As the war dragged on, Stöver no longer allowed people to buy fruit. Each family came to the factory with their own container and bought marmalade already made.

People made their own noodles, and sometimes fried potato pancakes. If they didn't have enough lard or butter, they browned grated raw potatoes anyway. These weren't too bad if you added a little marmalade or syrup. It filled you up. Lots of people wrapped fried potato cakes in paper and brought them to work for lunchtime. Maria couldn't eat them, however. She always said they tasted burnt.

The berry pickers ate everything they could pick during the harvest. The women working in the vegetable fields would fill up their blouses when the vegetables were ready. The ladies with big bosoms got away with a lot more, since they had the room.

For the entire six years of the war, Mother never ate her margarine ration. She always saved it for us because we were working and needed the calories. The only time I saw her have any margarine was when she made sandwiches for us. She would wipe the knife on a slice of bread and eat that. We said, "Mother, you get the ration too. Eat some of it."

She always said, "You need it more than I do. You have to walk to work. I don't need so much."

Even though I was still quite young, I had already developed a taste for coffee. However, under the Nazis, Poles didn't get a coffee ration. Each family was allotted a pound of ground rye per month to toast and brew into ersatz coffee. Some people dug dandelion roots which they cut into pieces, dried and roasted, and added to the rye to improve the taste. Sometimes we could get real tea and most women were adept at making their own herbal teas out of plants they gathered. We particularly enjoyed a tea my aunts made from linden tree blossoms.

We thought about food constantly during those hungry years. Sometimes we reminisced about the abundance we'd enjoyed before the occupation. We retold the stories of Slawa smuggling the sausages around her waist and Mother locking the *Burgermeister* in the smokehouse. Remembering feasts and laughter cheered us and we thanked God for our family and relative security at Pudliszki.

*   *   *

German citizens also had to use ration books and stamps. Our German Uncle Hans had been good friends with many of the local German families. He came from Berlin for a visit early in the war because he thought he might be able to use his connections to help our family. His German friends all told him there was nothing they could do—they were also subject to rationing and agricultural inspection. One farmer told him, "Hans, imagine this. I can't even kill my own pig anymore!"

Tina's work pass book. Everyone had to carry passes at all times.

Clothing was another thing that was rationed and fabric was difficult to obtain. Mother was a talented seamstress, and she became a wheeler-dealer in the black market even after the Gestapo confiscated her sewing machine. This came about through her friendship with two German women in Krobia whom she had known since their school days together. The German women had left Krobia when Poland became independent and they had sold their fabric shop to some Polish people. They returned after Germany occupied Poland, and the Poles sold the shop back to them. The women paid full price for the business, which was decent of them, since they could have asked for the business to be confiscated and awarded to them instead. Those women did well for themselves regardless, since they had black market dealings in fabric and clothing with most of the Germans.

One year, just before Easter, I went with Mother to the German fabric shop. Mother winked and said, "I really need some fabric for a blouse for my daughter and undershirts for my son."

The women said, "Do you have ration stamps for that? Come into the shop for some tea."

We went into the back, and Mother said, "Could you use any eggs?" She knew that even the Germans had trouble getting eggs, and she also knew the women wanted to bake special Easter cakes. Mother traded a package of eggs for the cloth she wanted.

The women said, "Here is your receipt to show that you had proper ration stamps. Remember, if anyone asks you, say of course you had the stamps."

Everything was bought and sold on the black market. The Germans were issued more stamps than we were, but it was still difficult for them to buy clothing. The Neugebauer family traded their farm products for fabric and then had my mother or another seamstress sew for them. The fabric shop women always knew a deal could be made when someone came into their shop with a bag or package. If the shop was full of people, they would wait until it cleared out, then make the trade. They were sharp.

Tina and Andrzej Jurkowski and Marina Bartlic at Easter, 1944. The girls are wearing coats with fur collars and muffs. They had to hide the furs for the duration of the war, since it had been requisitioned for the military, but they wore them briefly during our Easter celebration.

Stöver knew all about the black market. He called it *UDT,* for *Unter den Tisch* (Under the Table). He said, "Just look at them — look at my German people. Even with rationing, they still get anything they want. I know what the allowances are and how much everyone makes, and yet they have everything!" Of course, his wife had everything she wanted too. *Frau* Stöver was always elegantly dressed in fine clothes and nice shoes. She traded with the same German women in Krobia and sent the fabric to be sewn in Berlin. She would say, "Oh, I bought this when I visited my mother," or "My mother sent this to me," but we all knew what she was doing. Stöver just winked at her complicity. Of course, he was doing the same thing himself, bartering and trading on the black market for all the goods his family wanted. He had fine tastes himself. He proudly showed off his Leica camera, and bragged about how complicated it was to operate, even though most fine optical equipment like his camera had been requisitioned for the German war effort.

*   *   *

During the occupation, the Pudliszki factory began making dehydrated potatoes. A group of captured English soldiers had been carrying rations that included dried potato flakes. The Germans had never seen these before, but quickly understood their value to the military. Dried potato flakes cooked quickly, they were light, and freezing conditions didn't hurt them, so they were easy to transport and use. The engineers at Pudliszki developed a dehydration process and the plant that made them worked day and night. The potatoes weren't even peeled. The product was intended for the military, but all the local Germans wanted some, both for themselves and to send to their families back in Germany. Stöver said, "Nothing doing. These are solely for the war effort, and no one else is to have them."

Frau Fischer protested, "But *Frau* Stöver told me your family ate them."

Stöver said, "Well, naturally, I had to sample them and make sure they were properly prepared. We only tried them one time."

Then *Frau* Stöver's family came from Berlin to visit. Right in front of everyone, *Frau* Stöver's mother said, "Oh, my dear Charlotte, thank you for sending us those dried potato flakes. They are just wonderful! They are delicious, and they cook so fast! Everyone in Berlin wants them, so we have been trading them for lots of other things." *Frau* Stöver grew completely red in the face and tried to shush her mother, but it was too late—the cat was already out of the sack. We Poles didn't care, because what could we do about it? Report it? To whom? We weren't that foolish. The incident demonstrated yet again that Stöver was as hypocritical as the rest of the Gestapo, treating himself and his family to the best of everything.

Mother always said, "Andrzej, that's how they are. Forget about it. It's nice that he tries to help his family. Remember, Ludwig was just trying to help his family. If Zosia hadn't been stupid and informed the police, he wouldn't have been killed."

*   *   *

Our apartment in the Kokoszki barracks was right outside the Pudliszki factory gates. The barracks were intended for Polish farm workers but during the middle of the war, some buildings were fenced off with wire so they could be used to house Allied POWs. These men had been shot down, taken prisoner, and then put to work in Pudliszki's fields. They marched three or four miles to work and back every day, and their route led right past our flat. As POWs, they were supposed to be receiving aid parcels from the Red Cross but the packages were usually stolen before reaching their intended recipients. The prisoners were fed only bread and water, and not much of that, and no one was permitted to approach them. They looked so hungry that my sisters and their girlfriends decided to help. The girls put bread in the bodices of their blouses, moved among the marching men as they passed, and handed out the bread. It worked the first time because the guards were taken unaware. When the girls tried the trick again, the guards knocked them down and beat them with the butts of their rifles. Despite their beatings, the girls waited a week and tried a third time, but the guards were ready for them and beat them before they could get close enough to pass along any food.

The military prisoners were transferred elsewhere, and Jewish prisoners were brought in. One evening during the tomato season, a man came to the door of our apartment. At the time, we were all sitting in the dark because of the nightly blackout, but what I could see of him shocked me. My God, I had never seen such a skinny human being. He said to Mother, "*Pani*, please help me. I am Jewish. We are starving to death." Mother gave him bread and as many tomatoes as he could put down his shirt. Then he ran back to his barracks. He came back several times. We had to warn him, "Don't tell anyone who gave you this," because we would have been shot. There was no tolerance for helping the Jews, but we did what we could.

*   *   *

Stöver wanted the Pudliszki workers to be productive. He said, "My people must work. They need to be productive because I need to fill my orders. I need them healthy." He did not allow the workers to be mistreated, but he didn't ask how much food they were getting either. Stöver had a series of German overseers directing the farm operations, and the work crews were supervised by German agricultural bosses, but most of these people lasted only a month or two in their jobs. If they rocked the boat in any way—and sooner or later they always did— Stöver transferred them.

One of the German overseers was a man named Weiss. He was a Nazi true-believer, unlike Stöver who played the part of Nazi more out of self-interest rather than philosophical conviction. Weiss lobbied Stöver to change the factory's name from Pudliszki to something more German, so it became *Grosse Gärten* (Great Gardens). A late cold snap in the spring of 1940 froze many of the orchard trees down to the ground and they completely failed to bloom that year. Weiss was convinced that the farm workers had somehow sabotaged the orchards and threatened to execute them all in retribution. He even threatened to execute *Pan* Bartlic, the Polish chief agronomist. Stöver intervened, telling Weiss that nature had killed the trees, not treachery. Stöver protected his Polish laborers because he knew he needed workers.

The main labor force at Pudliszki was made up of 150 young Polish women who worked in the fields and factories. They were divided into work squads, each with a leader, with a *Hauptmädchen* (head girl) over them all. The women labored in the fields every day from six in the morning until six at night, with a half day off on Sunday. They walked for an hour from their barracks to their work and another hour back home in the evening. During the long days of summer, overseer Weiss decided he could increase production by forcing the women to work an extra two hours each day. He told the women they were now required to work from 6 a.m. until 8 p.m., even though all Poles had an 8 p.m. curfew. On the first night of the new hours, as the women were walking back to their barracks well after 8 o'clock, the police showed up and demanded to see their passes for breaking curfew. Of course, the women had no passes and the police arrested them. Some of the women were beaten and the squad leaders who argued with the police were thrown in jail overnight.

I was at my desk outside Stöver's office the next morning when the police reported the arrests. Stöver was furious with Weiss and called him every dirty name he could think of. He told Weiss that his job was to follow orders, not give them. "Do you think the fields work themselves? You cost us several days of production and I had a lot of trouble getting the squad leaders out of jail."

Stöver had little interest in caring for the workers as fellow humans. He was interested only in saving his own skin by meeting his production targets. He treated the workers as business assets and tried to keep the enterprise operating smoothly.

Stöver planned to transfer Weiss to the front after his curfew stunt. However, Weiss was suddenly diagnosed with an aggressive cancer and couldn't leave Pudliszki. Weiss had a deep hatred for religion and a particular dislike of nuns, but the cancer diagnosis changed his tune. He ordered Sister Helena to sit with him and pray the rosary around the clock. If he couldn't hear her praying day and night, he became enraged. He would say, "I don't care if it's twenty-four hours a day. That doesn't interest me. You have to pray for me so I don't die."

Sister Helena didn't even get a break to go to the bathroom until *Frau* Weiss offered to sit with her husband. After a week, Stöver asked me where Sister Helena was. I told him she was sitting with Weiss and praying. Stöver went to Weiss's house and thanked the nun. He said, "I think you are a good person and you have done a good thing by praying for him. That man is a no-good bum." Sister Helena couldn't reply, because what could a Polish nun say to an SS officer?

*   *   *

The rationing system was typical of the elaborate Nazi bureaucracy. At Pudliszki, Stöver hired *Fraulein* Neugebauer, the daughter of the amiable German colonist, *Herr* Neugebauer, to distribute the ration stamps. She worked from a list that detailed how the stamps were to be disbursed to all of Kokoszki's residents, including the farm laborers. At first, *Fraulein* Neugebauer had German assistants, but they had been transferred to other offices or drafted into the army as the war went on.

In 1943, Stöver assigned me to be her rationing assistant. I was eighteen by then, and my new duty made me quite apprehensive, since I knew that if any problems arose, I would get the blame.

Fraulein Neugebauer remembered me and my family from before the war, and we got on well together. She was a kind woman, so I was hopeful she would not make trouble for me in my new job. She assigned me a desk in the nearly empty office and gave me the ration stamp distribution list. I was to mark off on the list how many stamps each person or family received, count out all the stamps and put them into labelled envelopes, and then tell her I had distributed them appropriately. I realized right away that I could cheat by giving out extra stamps. The responsibility scared me to death. If I were caught giving out extra stamps, I would be sent to a concentration camp or even executed right there. But I realized I could also do some good. With this in mind, I started dividing up my first sheet of stamps—a sheet for sugar. I knew that sugar was the most important thing for the young women living in the farm barracks and working in the fields for twelve hours a day. They weren't getting enough calories and they were gradually starving. I decided to steal the whole goddamn sheet.

The leaders of the work squads brought me lists of their crews so I could count out a stamp for each worker. I knew one of the crew leaders, so I spoke to her privately, saying, "I've found some extra sugar stamps, and I know I can trust you. But can I trust the other leaders?"

She said, "Andrzej, there's no problem. No one will talk. The workers are already stealing all the food they can just to stay alive."

I began handing out a few extra stamps at a time after warning the leaders to tell the women to be careful and not buy a lot of sugar at once. They needed to spread their purchases out over several days and buy only one pound at a time. The storekeepers never questioned the purchases because they were getting the stamps. Of course, it was dangerous because if I had been caught it would have been all over for me and probably for my family, too. My brother Wojciech would have had a fit if he had known what I was doing. My sisters Maria and Tina were aware of what I was up to and they encouraged me. I never took anything for my family because we were doing all right, thanks to Mother and her connections with her well- placed German friends. She knew how to work the system.

After I successfully pilfered the sugar stamps, I gained a little confidence. I kept on distributing "extra" stamps every month, while I worked on getting ration coupons for shoes for the field workers. They needed shoes desperately, but we all did. My own shoes were clogs that I had made by taking apart some old shoes. The soles had worn through, so I took the uppers and nailed them onto carved wooden soles. I made the insoles from an old felt hat. The field workers tried to make similar clogs, but they had a terrible time out in the muddy fields in old broken shoes and wooden clogs. I knew this because my own sister Maria wore similar clogs to work in the market garden.

I told *Fraulein* Neugebauer that the work crews hadn't received ration stamps for shoes in more than two years. She advised me to ask

Stöver about it. I did, and he told me not to bother him with nonsense and sent me back to *Fraulein* Neugebauer. I said, "Stöver told me to ask you for coupons for shoes. How many will you give me?"

Fraulein Neugebauer asked, "Well, how many do you need?"

I replied, "One hundred and fifty young women live in the barracks. If I can get fifty pairs this month, and fifty more for each of the next two months, they will be set." Then I went to tell Stöver what I had asked for. Stöver called in the *Hauptmädchen*, and asked her why she hadn't reported that the workers had no shoes. She told him that she had been afraid to ask.

Stöver said, "If they are working, they must have shoes." He told the *Hauptmädchen* that the women would be issued the appropriate stamps and that a few women could go each day to buy shoes.

The requests continued. The squad leaders asked me for soap. Our family soap ration was for a bar of soap similar to Fels Naphtha each month. This cleaned quite well, even in cold water. However, the farm workers were not issued a soap ration, even though they were doing hard manual labor. Nothing is worse than having to put on filthy, sweaty clothes day after day, especially in cold weather, since dirty clothes don't provide any warmth. So I stole stamps for soap. The farm workers were overjoyed! Once they had soap, the women washed their clothes as quickly as they could, wrung them out well, and hung them by the stove to dry overnight.

Then the workers needed winter coats. Their clothes were rotting on their bodies. I went back to *Fraulein* Neugebauer and she said, 'Well, what do your lady friends need now?"

I said, "They are not MY lady friends. They work and they need what everyone needs."

Fraulein Neugebauer said, "I was just joking. My clothes are wearing out and I just sit in an office all day. I grew up on a farm and I know what physical labor is like. I can give you twenty-five clothing stamps every two weeks and eventually everyone will have a new coat." I bowed and kissed her hand and thanked her profusely. She said, "*Du bist ein guter Mensch.*" (You are a good person.)

The workers asked their leaders, "How did you get the soap, the shoes, the extra sugar? Where are these extra stamps coming from?" The leaders told the workers they were being rewarded for their hard work and that's why they were getting soap and shoes. No one betrayed me.

*   *   *

I had to take my chances and manipulate the stamps when I saw my own sister Maria dressed in rags while she marched to work in the fields every day with a hoe or a spade. Mother repaired Maria's clothes as well as she could, but they were patch on top of patch. But how could the poor women in the barracks sew anything? They were exhausted when they came home from work at night, and they had little light in the barracks. All the women slept in rows of bunk beds in a single long room. A pot-bellied stove sat in the middle of the room, and they heated their food on an old-fashioned wood stove at one end. They had only three kerosene lamps for the whole place, and they lit only one lamp at a time because their kerosene ration was not enough to burn all three lamps every night for a whole month. These days, people complain about the smell of kerosene, but at least a kerosene lamp gives off a little heat. You don't smell it when you need the light and the warmth. I asked *Fraulein* Neugebauer for an additional kerosene ration and told her to ask Stöver if she was unsure.

She said, "Oh, I don't need to ask Herr Stöver if you're sure he'll say yes." Then she gave me extra stamps for their kerosene.

*　　　　　　　*　　　　　　　*

Sometimes when we killed a rabbit, Mother would say, "Now this one has to go to Frusia." Frusia was an elderly lady with no children who had worked at Pudliszki her entire life. Long before the war, she got paid to sweep the streets around the mansion. She cleaned up horse and cattle manure and put it in a cart to sell for fertilizer. Frusia lived alone in a little hut. By now, she was well into her eighties and too old to work anymore, or even to cook for herself, so people brought her food.

One day Frusia came to the factory office cursing at the Germans in mumbled Polish. My desk was outside Stöver's office and he often had me interpret for him. Frusia marched straight into Stöver's office and started to harangue him in Polish. Her bad language scared me to death. Stöver called me in, saying, "Andreas, there's a crazy old lady in here! What does she want? What is she mumbling about?"

I went in and Frusia said to me in Polish, "What do I want? I want that damn German to give me food coupons. I am hungry. I want sugar, more sugar."

Stöver asked, "What's she saying?" I thought to myself, I hope he didn't understand the few words she used at the beginning.

"*Herr* Stöver, she is just asking for one extra sugar coupon."

"Why? What in hell does she need sugar for? She's old. She doesn't need all that energy!"

"*Herr* Stöver, please, can't you give her one?"

He looked at me and said, "Okay, the next time you fill out the *Lebensmittel* cards, you can give her an extra ration."

I told Frusia, "*Herr* Stöver tells me the next time I bring the stamps, you will get one extra."

She replied in Polish, "*Dzęnki Bogu* (Thanks be to God)."

Stöver looked at me, and asked, "What did she say?"

I answered, "She says, 'Thanks to be to God.'"

He said, "Tell her the sugar didn't come from God! She should be thanking me!"

Frusia asked, "What did he say?"

She got confused when I told her Stöver said she should thank him instead of God. She started mumbling and cursing the Germans again. I told Stöver I couldn't understand what she was saying. He said, "Okay, just get her out of here." I took her by the hand and led her away. I was always nervous when he got angry.

*   *   *

We were all fortunate that Stöver delegated the responsibility of issuing stamps to me. I am sure he did it by design. His primary concern was to keep the plant operating smoothly. I believe Stöver expected me to steal extra stamps to help the workers. When he told me to give that extra sugar stamp to old Frusia, I was sure he knew I was manipulating the stamps. Making extra rations available helped keep the laborers healthy enough to work and kept Pudliszki's production high. Stöver knew he wouldn't be blamed if Gestapo inspectors discovered any discrepancies — it would all be blamed on me, and I would take the punishment.

One of Stöver's German assistants was *Herr* Schmidt, an officious little man who was barely five feet tall. Schmidt was married, but I often heard him making advances toward the women who worked in the office. Most of them rebuffed him, although one woman began to carry on an affair with him. She was *Fraulein* Herbst, a tall, robust young Amazon. Schmidt's head barely reached her bosom, and people joked that he enjoyed the comfort and convenience. *Fraulein* Herbst was a notorious flirt and she enjoyed teasing Schmidt by making eyes at other men. She tried to provoke him by flirting with me right in front of him. This infuriated him, because I was just a scrawny Polish kid of eighteen. Schmidt lost all control. He called me into the garden, pulled out a pistol, and threatened to shoot me dead if I ever spoke to *Fraulein* Herbst again. He blustered and foamed as he waved the pistol around. I was terrified, but I tried to reassure him that I would never make advances toward a German woman and eventually he let me go. The whole office knew what had happened except for Stöver, until one of the senior secretaries told him about it. Stöver called me in for questioning and I had to tell him the whole story. Once again, Stöver was furious with one of his German employees for disrupting Pudliszki's operations. Schmidt was transferred immediately. The entire office staff was lectured about their lack of discipline, although Stöver told me in private that he knew the incident was not my fault. I appreciated his understanding, but it was small consolation for having to face a madman with a loaded pistol.

*　　　　　　*　　　　　　*

Our daily life working for Stöver at Pudliszki was stable compared to many other places. This made it possible for some people to aid the resistance efforts that were being organized by leaders of the Polish army who had not been taken prisoner in the early part of the war. A few young people were approached about joining resistance efforts, but everything was secret. My brother Wojciech was privy to some operations, but he kept his mouth shut. He had been promoted to Pudliszki's head bookkeeper, and as he was given more responsibility, he could delay orders and requests from the military. Because I worked directly for Stöver, I was often able to hold back letters as they came and went. I delayed enough to slow things down without his realizing. People did what they could to hinder the Nazi war effort without being obvious about it.

Early in the war, the German administration named *Pan* Bartlic to be the director of both the Pudliszki agricultural operations and the canning factory. *Pan* Bartlic had a doctorate in agronomy. Before the war, he had been the chief agronomist on another agricultural estate. He scheduled the seeding, fertilizing, and harvest, and planned the crop rotation. *Pan* Bartlic was a strict manager and Stöver trusted him, because if *Pan* Bartlic ordered a job to be done, it was done well.

My best friend at that time was *Pan* Bartlic's son, Jurek, who worked in the canning factory. He told me that the machinery was operating continuously and that it frequently broke down, causing production delays. One day, Stöver asked Jurek why the machines were always breaking down. Jurek told him, "Our equipment is running around the clock and it's already old. When something breaks, we need to send out for a special mechanic to fabricate a new part. This takes time."

Stöver asked Jurek, "Why don't you tell me what's going to break before it happens, so we can order the parts ahead of time?"

Jurek laughed and replied, "I can't predict what will break next. I only know after it's broken."

Stöver said, "Ah, well, I hadn't thought about that."

This remark revealed that Stöver didn't have a technical understanding of how the factory operated. Arranging for the mechanic to come to Pudliszki always took a couple of days, and while the delay infuriated Stöver, he didn't doubt that *Pan* Bartlic was running the factory as efficiently as possible. Stöver never learned that calls to the mechanic didn't go out right away.

*　　　　　　　*　　　　　　　*

The Pudliszki factory processed all the fruit grown on the estate. In addition, we received trainloads of fruit for canning from all over Europe. Pudliszki had its own railway spur which enabled huge barrels of dried peaches, pears, and apricots packed in sulfur to be unloaded directly at the factory. One day Jurek opened one of the barrels and found human remains mixed in with the fruit. He called for Stöver to come right away. Stöver peered into the barrel and said, "What is it? I don't see anything." Jurek stirred around with a paddle, then Stöver saw a hand and an arm with an SS tattoo and number on it. Stöver was sick. Then he ordered the workers to open the rest of the barrels and they found the remains of two more SS men. Stöver called the *Gauleiter* in Poznan and an investigation found that Italian resistance fighters had been ambushing individual Gestapo men when they were alone and unprotected. The victims were strangled and dumped into the barrels of preserved fruit. The barrels sat around for a while before being shipped to us so there was no way to investigate murders, and we never heard an official report.

View of fruit barrels from Pudliszki tower, 1944

Episodes like this strengthened Stöver's resolve to stay safely at Pudliszki where he was surrounded by relatively docile Poles, and his determination grew as the Allied bombardment of Berlin intensified. He knew Berlin was no refuge. His wife's home there was destroyed in late 1943. The bombing crews had been aiming at the Kaiserhof Hotel, where many important Gestapo officers lived. I saw the ruins of the hotel when I visited Berlin in 1945, and I was shocked to see such a massive building split wide open. The bombs also fell on the suburb of Charlottenburg, where Frau Stöver's family lived. Her elderly parents were saved, although her sister lost a leg when the apartment building collapsed.

Stöver never looked too deeply into the perpetual delays and breakdowns. Often ten or twelve railroad cars waited on the spur track for several days until a locomotive came to take the cars away. Almost every month, saboteurs mined the tracks somewhere along the line and a train would be blown up. The newspapers never wrote about sabotage and Stöver never mentioned it. The Gestapo took their revenge on people near where the explosions occurred. They never came after the people at Pudliszki, even though it was our factory workers who had alerted the resistance with information about the shipments. No one ever talked about it — people kept their mouths shut.

*   *   *

My friend Jurek became aware of a national underground resistance organization when his aunt told him about the *Armija Krajona* (AK), the Army of the Country. I had already heard rumors about the AK. Their forces were sabotaging transportation all over the country, dynamiting railroad tracks, blowing up bridges, and so forth. The AK aimed to delay the transport of soldiers to the front and disrupt shipments of supplies, ammunition, and food. Jurek and I agreed that we had to be very careful and never talk about any of this. We knew the AK executed anyone detected who informed on them and even anyone who discussed their actions.

The Polish Resistance was obsessive about internal security. *Pan* Chmielowski had been the pharmacist in Krobia, but he and his family moved to Warsaw when the Germans closed the pharmacy. His son wanted to join the Resistance even though he was only fourteen years old. An AK representative went to his parents and said, "You know that if he is caught, he will be beaten and tortured. Will he betray us? Or will he be willing to die? Because if he wants to join us, he cannot betray us." The Chmielowkis swore that he would never betray the resistance. A year or so later, the boy was caught and tortured. He broke down and told his interrogators everything he knew. When the Gestapo released him, the AK executed him right on the street.

I lost other friends in resistance operations. The Anziewski family from Gostyn had twin boys my age. When the war started, the family moved to Warsaw, where the boys joined the Resistance. They had a dirty job—they threw homemade bombs at truckloads of soldiers. They were lucky and didn't get caught for three years, but in the end, one of the bombs didn't go off and they were captured. The soldiers put the boys against the nearest wall and shot them dead in the street. They were buried where they fell and they lie there still. Their parents were beside themselves with grief. That's how life was in those days.

At the end of the war, my friend Jurek said to me, "Remember when we talked about the Resistance and how we could never discuss it? What did you think about what we went through?"

All I could say was, "Thanks be to God that we were lucky. So many others were not."

Jurek and Andreas at Pudliszki, 1944

9. The Last Days of the Nazis

Early in the spring of 1944, an elderly Polish man came into Stöver's office. He was trying to speak German, but Stöver yelled to me, "Andreas! Come here and tell me what this old fool wants. I can't understand him." I listened. The man was excited and wanted to share his good news. He had observed a flock of storks returning to their nesting places in the woods for the first time since the beginning of the war. In Poland, the springtime arrival of the storks is an omen of prosperity and fertility. Everyone rejoices to see them. I told Stöver that the old man was trying to tell him that the storks had returned. Stöver said, "What the hell do I care about storks? Get him out of here!" I had no reply, but my heart lifted at thought of the storks' return.

By June of 1944, we could tell that things were going badly for the Germans. The Allies had opened the western front after D-Day and were advancing across France. The Soviet Army was forcing the Germans to retreat on the eastern front. The Gestapo had ordered all the church bells taken down and melted for use in armaments. The troops being sent to the east were either old men or *Hitlerjugend* (Hitler Youth) who were barely teenagers. We began to hope that the end was coming. Stöver began sending me up in the factory's tower to watch for Allied bombers. When I heard them, I was supposed to call to the office and warn Stöver to take shelter. I knew this was a foolish idea, because by the time I could hear the planes they were already past us, but it made Stöver feel safer. Every time I called him with a warning, he ran like a gazelle to his bomb shelter in the woods. I wondered how Stöver was always the first one to the shelter, until my brother told me about his athletic career before the war. What a hero.

After living in Pudliszki's mansion for most of the war, Stöver and his family moved into a smaller house on the estate's grounds. Stöver liked to do things his own way and as the military situation deteriorated, he didn't want a spy on the staff reporting back to the *Gauleiter* or to Berlin about his involvement in the black market, or anything else that might get him transferred to a combat position. He was the big boss, so he could do what he wanted. The German Director of Agriculture continued to live in the mansion where my sister Tina still managed the kitchens.

Before the war, Tina had been engaged to a young man named Tadeusz Kosciuszko. He was a direct descendent of the Tadeusz Kosciuszko who was a hero of the American revolutionary war. Tina's Tadeusz had been taken prisoner during the early stages of the war, and after a year or so Tina learned that he was alive and in a POW camp in Germany. The Gestapo permitted Tina to send him boxes of food supplies — two kilos every six months. When the Agricultural Director heard that Tina was supporting an enemy of Germany, he let the Gestapo conscript her to dig trenches for the retreating German army. Stöver was angry when he learned she'd been taken, but it was too late to save her.

Tina was conscripted when she was twenty-seven, and she spent almost a year away from us. She was part of a prisoner brigade assigned to work alongside soldiers at the front. The Germans didn't care if their prisoners lived or died, and didn't provide them with food or supplies. Tina volunteered to cook for her crew because she knew how to cook for a large group. When horses that pulled the German artillery were killed in battle, Tina ran out with a butcher knife to cut off chunks of meat. She cooked the horsemeat over an open fire and that food was enough for the prisoners to survive on. Her crew told her that her cooking was wonderful and asked how she made the meat so tasty and sweet. Tina would reply, "It's only natural, because everything I do is sweet."

The Germans withdrew in the face of Soviet shelling and were eventually forced to make a rapid retreat. Tina and her team were overrun by the Soviet artillery and put to work digging trenches for them. It was the same work for different masters. The Soviet pursuit of the Germans proceeded so rapidly that conscripts couldn't keep up with the rapidly advancing front. Finally, a Soviet commander told the Polish prisoners to go home. It took Tina took several months to get back to us. Along the way, she was raped by a Russian soldier and became pregnant. Unlike many others, she was not killed.

Meanwhile, Tadeusz had fallen in love with one of the Polish women in his prison camp. When she became pregnant, he married her. After the war, he came back to Pudliszki to thank Tina for sending the food supplies that had helped him survive, and to explain about marrying another woman. Tina said, "Tadeusz, don't apologize. Look what happened to me. I also have a child—I have my daughter, you have your daughter, and we will just go our own ways. Good luck to you, my friend."

*   *   *

I was working at the switchboard early in January of 1945 when *Gauleiter* Greiser in Poznan telephoned Stöver. I connected him and as the two men began to talk, I listened instead of hanging up. *Gauleiter* Greiser said, "Get all the Germans together. The Russians are right on our backs and you need to evacuate everyone to Germany, now. You can take any

Poles who want to go with you, if you want to." I thought to myself, well, *Herr Gauleiter*, you have a lot of nerve to start worrying about the Poles now.

Stöver's wife was the head typist in our office. The *Gauleiter* was aware of this, so then he said, "Before you leave, I want *Frau* Stöver to make a list of the names of all of the Polish men at Pudliszki over the age of sixteen. Leave it on your desk. The SS will come for that list within twenty-four hours of your departure." We had already heard that the SS were killing men in other parts of Poland to prevent the Russians from conscripting them into the Russian army. The SS surrounded towns and villages, herded all the men inside churches and other large buildings, and torched them. Then they stood around the edges with machine guns and shot everyone who tried to flee the flames. If you didn't run, you burned up.

After Stöver and his wife left the office to prepare for departure, I went in and took the list off Stöver's desk. It's too damn bad I didn't keep it, because it would have been war crime evidence at the Nuremburg trials. I showed the list to my brother and then we burned that piece of shit. But even after Stöver fled and the list was destroyed, the fear remained. The men of Krobia and Kokoszki spent the bitter January nights in barns and in shelters in the woods in case the SS came for them. We had luck on our side though, because they never came.

Stöver commandeered the estate's Mercedes and a truck from the factory. He had workers load the truck with tons of canned food along with all his possessions, and then he told the rest of the Germans that he had received his orders. They, too, needed to pack and go. I remember that *Frau* Fischer, said, "I want that truck, because my husband was killed on the Russian front, and I am entitled to a ride."

Stöver looked her right in the eye, and said, "*Heil* Hitler. I am the SS and I have the first right to the truck. You will get beautiful horses and a wagon with a cover over it and there will be a man to accompany you wherever you want to go. I myself am going to Berlin."

Frau Meyer, the German woman who had moved into our farmhouse, packed her possessions and prepared to flee. Aunt Zofia came into the living room just as *Frau* Meyer was hurling a framed photograph of Hitler onto the floor. Zofia exclaimed, "What are you doing? Oh, dear, you broke Adolf into pieces!"

Frau Meyer said, "Yes, I was rushing to pack." But then Zofia watched her go from room to room throwing all her Hitler photographs on the floor. She broke the glass and stomped on the pictures. *Frau* Meyer looked at Zofia and said, "This is just not right. We shouldn't have to leave. He promised us everything! Why didn't he keep his promise?"

Zofia said, "I can't answer you. You need to ask him yourself. Why don't you telephone *der Führer* in Berlin and ask him what happened?"

Once *Frau* Meyer was gone, Mother, Maria, and I moved from the Kokoszki apartment back into our farmhouse with our aunts and uncles.

Stöver left in the Mercedes with his wife, his son Jürgen, and his son's nursemaid—a Polish girl from Krobia named Marina. Two local boys, Nowak and Jabodinski, accompanied Stöver, driving the factory's truck packed with canned food. Stöver might have told people he was headed for Berlin, but his little convoy headed west as fast and as far as they could. I think Stöver intended to surrender to the Americans. They had almost reached Magdeburg, west of Berlin, when Stöver realized the Russians were too close for him to escape. He stopped in a small village where he bribed the local people not to denounce him. He paid his Polish drivers to attest to the Communists about his benevolent administration of Pudliszki. Stöver, his family, and his three Polish attendants settled in the village and lived for several years off the food he had stolen.

Stöver's maid Marina was friends with *Pan* Bartlic's daughter, Barbara, back in Pudliszki. Marina wrote Barbara about life in East Germany, while Barbara wrote back about the harsh demands the Communists were making of the Poles. Marina and the two drivers stayed in East Germany with Stöver for more than two years. All three Poles decided they preferred life there, until the Communist government eventually pressured Stöver to send them home.

Like many Nazi officers, Stöver was an able administrator and an adept politician — he didn't stay down for long. His talents were recognized, and he eventually became the *Burgermeister* of his village.

In 1950, Stöver and his wife paid a visit from East Germany to Krobia while on vacation. He had heard rumors that productivity at the Pudliszki factory had fallen, largely due to Communist mismanagement and corruption. Stöver still had a reputation for effective management and there was a lot of sympathy between the East German and Polish Communists. He ingratiated himself with the Communist apparatchiks, and despite his wartime record as an SS officer, he was hired to manage the Pudliszki factory. He administered the factory for several years with some success, although other managers resented having a former Nazi officer promoted over them and began making trouble. Stöver didn't wait to be fired. He convinced the Communist policy makers in Warsaw that the entire factory needed to be disposed of.

In the late 1950's, Pudliszki was sold to the Gerber corporation. In 1997, Gerber resold it to Heinz who kept the name. Pudliszki remains a prestige brand of canned foods across Europe to this day.

    *   *   *

The Germans fought for almost a month in January of 1945 to defend Poznan from the advancing Soviet army. As house-to-house fighting broke out across the city, most civilians holed up in their basements. One of my cousins told me he and his family had survived by the same means as Tina. When a horse was killed, the people ran out and hacked off pieces. If they couldn't cook the meat, they minced it and ate it raw.

The winter of 1944-1945, which was particularly harsh across Europe, contributed to the deaths of thousands of civilians as well as military personnel. In Poznan, the bitter cold and lack of water were the worst parts of the civilian struggle during the month of heavy fighting. People had experience at coping with life in a war zone, so they knew to prepare for the ordeal by filling up every available container with water before the city water was shut off. They lived off the water they had saved in buckets and bathtubs, boiling it if they could. Electricity was shut off and the only light came from candles. Some people burned their furniture in little stoves made from oil drums, with stove pipes poking out the window.

As the Soviet army got closer to Krobia and Pudliszki, we heard terrifying rumors about their advance troops. These soldiers were reported to be Mongols mounted on huge motorcycles that were so loud they shook the earth. They were armed with machine guns and they wore bandoliers of bullets wrapped over their shoulders and around their waists. Usually two soldiers rode on the motorcycle, and sometimes they had a third in a sidecar. These men were impassive and merciless.

We heard the Soviet troops arrived in the town of Rawicz just as the Gestapo were preparing to massacre the Polish men. The Soviets shot every single German. The Gestapo begged for their lives, but there was no mercy for them. Some German units fought rearguard actions, as they did in Poznan, but as rumors spread, many Germans troops became demoralized and fled to Germany as fast as they could hobble. They believed that the Soviet troops took no prisoners but killed every German soldier they found.

The bitter cold continued into February and the soldiers of both armies suffered terribly. Night after night, small bands of German soldiers came to our house asking for food and a place to sleep. One night a group of four or five old soldiers and a couple of *Hitlerjugend* came to our door. They looked just like the men in the famous painting of Napoleon's soldiers retreating from Moscow. They were pathetic suffering humans—no longer agents of evil. Mother fed them soup and let them dry themselves by the kitchen stove. We were sitting quietly when a Gestapo officer rode up on a motorcycle and burst into the house. He looked over the sorry old men and the pitiful children and said, "*Heil* Hitler! How many of you are here? I have great news!" The old soldiers just looked at him until he glared at them and said, "*Heil* Hitler!" again.

They responded dully, "*Heil* Hitler."

The Gestapo officer said, "We've retaken Paris! We are advancing again to the east, and the war is almost over!"

The boys clapped in delight, crying, "That's wonderful! We knew it!" but the old soldiers just looked at one another in silence. After the officer left, they put their heads together muttering that of course it was all bullshit. No one could believe such lies. We knew it too. By February of 1945, the allies had broken free of the Battle of the Bulge and were approaching the Rhine.

One old soldier's feet were so frozen he could hardly walk. Mother offered to let him soak them in a basin of cool water. He said, "If I take my boots off, my feet will swell so much that the boots will never go back on."

Mother said, "I can dry your socks by the fire, and I have cardboard and sacking. We can make you some kind of covering to keep you going."

In the morning, the man's feet were swollen like balloons. He used the sacking and some rags to make coverings for his feet, and tied them on with his shoe laces. When he and his companions were leaving, he thanked Mother, and said, "I appreciate your help. I'm afraid we aren't going to get ten miles down the road before the Russians shoot us, and that's if we're lucky." His fears were justified. The Soviets caught up with them and shot them all, including the boys.

The next day I was in Krobia and saw the Mongol soldiers shooting German soldiers in the streets, in the way that a hunter picks off deer — *zzzt-zzzt*. The victims rolled over, twitched, and died. The Mongols searched our farm, declaring that if they found any hidden German soldiers, they would execute us all. Wojciech was at the office at Pudliszki when the Soviet troops came through. Some of the soldiers attempted to burn the entire complex before their commander stopped them, saying, "Are you stupid? Stop or I'll shoot you! This place is a factory for feeding the people, not something to destroy for no reason." The mansion and the factory were saved — and promptly taken over by the Communists.

PART III
1945-1949

10. The Communists Take Over

By late February of 1945, the Germans had retreated completely from our part of Poland and the Communists had taken control. These were both Russian *apparatchiki* and their Polish collaborators. Fighting continued to the west and the Soviet Army had yet to reach Berlin, but our area was relatively peaceful.

I was now nineteen years old. My teenage years, from 1939 to 1945, had been spent trying to survive an invading force whose goal was the annihilation of my country. I felt a turbulent mixture of relief and apprehension as the Russians began their own campaign to extinguish Polish identity. At first, it seemed as if our situation had somewhat improved. The Soviets merely wanted to turn Poles into good Communist workers. We were no longer threatened with extermination for being subhuman. Now we were part of the machinery of the Soviet Union, dedicated to providing our labor as Moscow dictated.

*   *   *

As soon as Krobia was secure, the Communists replaced the swastika flying from the *Ratusz* with the flag of the Soviet Union. My cousin Zosia, the same girl who had betrayed Uncle Ludwig, pulled the Soviet flag down and replaced it with the Polish flag. As she did, she yelled, "This is not the Soviet Union, this is Poland!" She and some friends sang a few hymns and patriotic songs. This was a dangerous move, because German and Russian forces were still fighting only a few miles to the west of Krobia. Soviet military police took Zosia and her friends to their headquarters and began to rough them up. Fortunately for her, an officer realized what was going on and intervened. Zosia told him, "We have waited and fought for six years to see our flag and now you've put yours up instead."

The officer said, "Well, you've learned something. Don't speak out against us, or it will be much worse for you." Then he let her go.

The labor brigades of young women at Pudliszki continued to live in the barracks, but now they worked for the Communists. The authorities seized and collectivized all of the private farms, putting Party members in charge. The German colonists were repatriated. *Herr* Neugebauer cried like a child when he was forced to leave his beautiful farm.

Poles who had been evicted from their estates and now hoped to return to them also had their dreams dashed by the Communists. When the Germans began their resettlement program during the war, an old widow near us, Countess Czartoryska, was sent to live in the General Government region of central Poland. Although Stöver had disapproved of the action at the time, he couldn't stop it. After the war, the Countess returned to her estate, coming all the way back in a horse-drawn cart. But there was no room for the old nobility after the Communists took over. They called the Countess an exploiter and told her she couldn't live in her mansion again. Before the war, the Polish nobility generally took good care of their farmworkers, much as *Dziadzia* had done. It helped that all classes shared a common religion and similar belief in moral behavior. The workers on Countess Czartoryska's estate had long memories and they came out to protect her. One family invited her to share their farmhouse and the Countess lived with them until she died.

*   *   *

The new Communist bosses placed a military officer in charge of the Pudliszki factory. They also installed a political officer and a production overseer to keep an eye on *Pan* Josef Bartlic, the Polish agricultural manager. All the farm workers underwent political reeducation. They were taught that everyone was equal under the Communist system. There were no more elites. Everyone was a *tovarisch* — a comrade. Because *Pan* Bartlic had a doctorate in agronomy, he had always been treated with respect, even by Stöver. After the Soviets took over, one of the dairymen, Isador, walked up and slapped him on the shoulder and said "Josef, we are all *tovarisch* now. Everyone is equal, *fsyo ravno.*" *Pan* Bartlic looked at him and said, "*Tak, tak*, yes, yes, Idi, we are indeed all equal. Just you wait."

During the German occupation, the dairymen had all received a special ration of milk and butter. As soon as the Communists took over, the special food allocations ended and the dairy workers got the same meager milk ration as everybody else. The larger war was still going on and all production was taken for the Soviet army. One afternoon, Isador noticed a man carrying home a bucket of milk. He hollered at the man, "At least under Hitler, my children got milk! I thought we were all equal, but you're getting milk and I'm getting nothing!" Unfortunately, the man turned out to be the Communist political officer and he reported Isador to the military police. Isador was called into the office to speak to the Commandant. The police worked him over until he was black and blue. That's how Isador found out what *fsyo ravno*, all equal, really meant.

Isador went to see *Pan* Bartlic and said, "*Pan* Josef, I've learned something. Now I realize the truth of your words and I apologize for my lack of respect."

Pan Bartlic said, "Idi, it's okay. We are indeed all equal, because we're all in the same boat now. You need to watch out. You will have the right to work like you did during Hitler's time. And when the war ends you'll be lucky if you even have milk to buy, because it's all going to go to the *apparatchiki*, the Communist bureaucrats."

Isador looked at him and said, "God damn it, how do you know this?"

Pan Bartlic replied, "Just you wait. This is how it will be." He was right—the only way a worker got anything was to steal it.

11. Polish Army Officer Candidate Training

My friend Tadeusz and I heard that the authorities planned to reopen the forestry institute. After working in an office for six years, I was thrilled at the thought of being able to have a career working outdoors after all. Tadeusz and I rode our bicycles thirty kilometers to the school. The principal was interviewing applicants and he already knew both of us. He told us right away that Tadeusz would be accepted into the program because he was the son of a farmer.

The principal interviewed Tadeusz while I waited in the outer room. Tadeusz came out of the room very happy because he'd been accepted. Then the principal called me in. He said, "Look, the Communists already know your father and uncles were Polish nationalists. They remember that your father was a commander during the uprising for Polish independence. Your cousin was just arrested for raising the Polish flag and singing nationalist songs. If you were to become a forester, you would have to carry a gun, and they won't allow that."

I said, "But my father has been dead since I was four years old. I was raised by my grandfather, who loved Kaiser Wilhelm."

The principal replied, "That doesn't matter to them. Your father fought not only against Kaiser Wilhelm but he also fought against the Communists. Poland is a Communist country now, so you can't go to a state institute. You will never be allowed to enroll."

Then I asked, "How did they even know about me? They've been here less than two months!"

"They have quite an organization. You'll be surprised how much they know."

I remembered Uncle Stan's words from the beginning of the war when he said, "There will be no end to this. The Russians want all of Poland back under their control. Once they reach Germany, it will be a hundred years before they leave. All of you young people should get the hell out of Poland and look for life elsewhere, because there will be no life for you here." I began to realize that I had no future in Poland.

*   *   *

Since I could not enroll at the forestry institute, I needed to find another occupation. Hearing that the Polish army was starting a new round of officer training, I went to the recruiting station, where a sergeant told me to catch a train from Poznan to a training camp near Warsaw. At the train station, I met a lot of other young men like myself. We were all naïve — convinced that we were headed to officer training to find careers and serve our country.

When we arrived at our destination, we formed into ranks, lining up in front of the Polish officer who came to meet us. He wore an immaculate pre-war uniform, with spotless white gloves, tall boots, and lots of braid. We expected him to greet us with a patriotic speech. Instead, after informing us we were no longer private citizens, he lectured us about everything that was wrong with the Polish Army. We stood there blinking in bewilderment while he yelled about corruption in the army and the end of Polish nationalism. That was the beginning of three months of propaganda intended to turn us into Soviet soldiers.

The next day we took the train east to a military base in the city of Lodz, which was a center for fabric manufacturing. After our arrival, we marched past a cathedral and across an open square to the barracks. I got off to a bad start with the officer in charge when I said, "Look, boys, the church is right across the square, so we won't have too far to walk on Sundays."

The officer took a hard look at me and said, "Of course, they have a special service that's just for soldiers like you boys."

Our training started. We got up in the morning and showered. That water was so cold! I could barely move when I got out, but there was nothing I could do about it, and I survived. Then we had breakfast— a thick piece of coarse bread with marmalade scraped over it. On Sundays, we got a little margarine as well. The main meal of the day was dinner—a pot of soup and a cup of coffee in the early afternoon. Of course, the coffee wasn't real coffee, just roasted barley with chicory in it. We called it chai-oo, fake tea. The soup always had plenty of cabbage, but the meat was chasing the meat, as they say, so I was lucky if I got any at all. The mess sergeant fussed around trying to make sure that every boy got at least four pieces of potato. For supper, we were given another piece of bread and more chai-oo.

The officer training academy had about 200 hundred cadets. We were divided into two battalions, and then split into platoons of about thirty and then further broken into squads of about fifteen. Every day, we sat through eight hours of classroom lectures. The mornings began with four hours of political theory and then we ate dinner. After dinner, the training continued with four hours of historical education. It was nothing but propaganda and the instructors were all NKVD, the Communist Party's secret police. We heard how in the new Poland we would have freedom of religion and freedom of expression. The head instructor was from Silesia, in the south of Poland, while most of the cadets were from the more northern districts of Poznan and Pomerania. Silesia had a different historical background from the rest of Poland, since it had been part of the Austro-Hungarian empire. Austrian and Czech influence were stronger there, while the northern and western districts had been ruled by Prussia and Germany. Even before the Soviets took over Poland, northern Poles didn't fully trust the Silesians, because we thought they had Communist tendencies. The boys from the southern part of Poland tended to be more insular than those of us from the north. The boys from Pomerania were very pro-German, while those of us from the Poznan district tended to be the most tolerant, since we all spoke both German and Polish. Everyone stayed within his own individual circle and we were all alert, sniffing for subtle clues about other people's thoughts and intentions.

Every day we listened to the instructors drone on about demolishing the insidious roots of capitalism permeating our society. The first lecture was about Kosciusko and Pulaski and the conquering of America. The instructors said things we knew were lies — that Kosciusko and Pulaski helped the Americans with their revolution because of the materialistic tendencies that were the result of their classist upbringings, and how the Americans exploited them. The instructors criticized Paderewski for negotiating Polish independence through Woodrow Wilson's peace terms at the end of World War I, and they told us how everything would have been much better if Poland had stayed a part of Russia. The instructors condemned everything that was American and English, and everything Polish as well. Every day we fell asleep in class. The instructor would yell, "I hear snoring! Wake up or it's extra marching!" That was a meaningless threat, since we got extra marching regardless of how many of us slept through the lectures.

The instructors emphasized how great an obligation we had to the new Communist government. They told us the government was more to us than our parents, because the government fed us, clothed us, housed us, and protected us. It was our obligation to report anything said against the government, no matter what relationship we had with the person. This was exactly like life under the Gestapo, when we were told to be thankful that Hitler was feeding us. This is the reason I don't understand how people can betray their families. I have seen for myself how governments come and go, but you are part of your family forever.

On our first Sunday, we asked when we could go to Mass. The officer in charge told us he didn't know what time the service was held, but he'd find out. He never did tell us, so we missed it. The officer had more excuses on the second and third Sundays, and we began to mutter out loud. The officers allowed us to attend Mass on one occasion, and then the schedule was changed so that Sunday became another work day and we were sent out to the firing range or on maneuvers. We attended Mass only twice in the whole three months of training. This disregard of our Catholic faith was an intentional assault on our Polish identity.

At that time, Stalin and the U.S. had supposedly agreed that fighters from the Polish Resistance would be given amnesty. We were assured that no retribution would be taken for resistance activities as the Soviet officers tried to get us to declare any roles we might have played during the war. We warned each other that this was probably a ploy to identify Polish nationalists. Our squad included five boys from Warsaw who had fought in the Warsaw uprising. They volunteered this information to the officers, even though we had warned them to keep quiet.

Nothing happened to the Warsaw boys until we began our field training after a few weeks of classroom lectures. Our group of forty cadets was sent out on live-fire exercises. The field was set up with a deep trench. We were supposed to lie behind sandbags at the edge of the trench, and on a signal, rush across and attack the enemy on the far side. We were positioned so that the five Warsaw boys were set at one end of the line, with an NKVD officer next to them. The order came to charge the trench. Then we heard *zzzt-zzzt-zzzt* and lots of shouting, "Stop the attack! Stop! We have an American spy among us! Someone has shot these boys!" Every one of the five Warsaw boys had been shot through the head.

We carried their bodies back to the barracks. The political officer organized a huge military funeral, and Marshal Rola-Zhimierski, Stalin's puppet leader of Poland, came in person to pin medals on the coffins to display Poland's love for the poor heroes murdered by western imperialists. We cadets agreed we could trust nobody and that no one would ever find out what the rest of us had done in the Resistance. Those Warsaw boys had fought for so long and so hard. They joined the army to continue serving their country and all they got were bullets in their heads. Their murders were an object lesson on the Communist policy towards Polish nationalism.

*   *   *

Our training session ended in June of 1945, and we prepared for our final testing by the NKVD officers. Every cadet who passed would be sworn in as an officer of the Polish army. He would get to carry a revolver and have a special leather strap on his uniform to show that he was a fully qualified officer. Not many of us passed the test. The instructors announced that we didn't do well enough. They told us they weren't surprised, because we hadn't tried very hard. Those of us who failed were transferred to a labor brigade to spend three months working under military command. We would be permitted to enroll again when the

next officer training class began its three-month course of political indoc-
trination. That's what they called it. Of course, we had all been investigated by the authorities during the training. The realization was dawn-
ing that because of our family backgrounds and war histories, none of
us would be allowed to have a military career.

12. Labor Camp

Rejected as officer candidates, my squad was marched away from the barracks to the yard of a textile factory complex. We were locked behind barbed wire fences with a group of other inmates who were mostly Russian soldiers. The officer in charge of us pointed down into a pit in the yard. It was the basement of a building that had been destroyed by Allied bombing. The officer said, "Here you go. You boys sleep down in this hole, on the cement."

We said, "We don't even get mattresses?"

He answered, "No, no. There's still a war going on, you know." A few of us put two of our military overcoats on the ground and we slept huddled together under the other coats. My little group was fortunate, because we were befriended by a veteran soldier, Sergeant Czeslof, a Ukrainian. A long and dark history of betrayal and murder lies between Poles and Ukrainians, so we didn't trust him at first, but he turned out to be our savior.

An older Polish Army captain gave our orientation when we arrived. He had survived World War I and then served time in a Siberian prison camp. When Stalin released the prisoners to join the Soviet army, the captain served under Soviet command. He spoke bluntly, saying "Boys, you better keep together. Watch out for each other, or these Russians will eat you right up to your hair."

We had started to wise up, so we looked at each other, thinking, "Can this guy really be saying these things about the Russians?" Soon after that, the officer disappeared. He was taken to headquarters and the Polish guards on the gates told us he was beaten and then executed.

Sergeant Czeslof asked us, "Did you hear what that officer said? Did you hear what happened to him?" We nodded, and Czeslof said, "Don't let that happen to you. Keep your stupid mouths shut. Someone in your ranks reported him and got a reward for it."

Every day an officer marched us from our yard into the city. Some days we cleared rubble from bombed buildings in the hot June sun. Other days we waited at the train station to unload cargo. In the evenings, we were marched back to our pit behind the wire. While we worked at the station, I saw terrible things — the monstrosity of war. Trainloads of wounded Russian soldiers were heading east. Among them were women soldiers with no feet and no legs, moaning, stinking from pee. Why were they kept alive? Some of the soldiers had been blinded. They had no faces, no hands. Some of the men had no legs, no testicles, no dicks. The heat was unbearable and the poor people were begging for water. We were told we would be shot if we gave them even a sip. People died in front of my eyes. Sergeant Czeslof told us that Stalin was shipping them home and letting them die along the way. He was using them as examples of cowards and traitors — of soldiers who were afraid to sacrifice their lives for the motherland. They were scapegoats.

We asked Sergeant Czeslof about the other men in our labor camp. He said, "Boys, if you look around, you'll see that most of the men in here are old Russian soldiers. They are veterans of six years of war. They fought from Leningrad to Minsk and then all the way to Berlin. Notice how they don't have any insignia on their uniforms? You can see the rips and tears where the badges and medals were. They got into trouble just for asking if they could have a furlough to go home and see their families. Most of those men had battle medals. Everything they had was ripped away. Now they have nothing and they will never get home. Stalin has declared them traitors because they asked for leave after five or six years of fighting. You watch what happens to them, and for God's sake, keep your mouths shut."

The Sergeant continued, "You boys are here for cleansing purposes. You'll never see that officer training school again. You were all investigated when you were in your first training class. They found out your histories and you were rejected. If you're lucky, you will get a transfer into the regular army and become a soldier somewhere. And if not..." He mimed a shot to the head.

We kept our eyes open. Every few days, a truck would come with some officers who had red tabs on their collars—they were the NKVD, the secret police. They loaded up some of the Russians soldiers, telling them they were being transported to another work site. None of the soldiers ever came back. One of our boys asked where the other work site was, and the officer said, "You'll see it soon enough. It's a lot better there, and those old guys are happy now." We discussed the Sergeant's words among ourselves. He had given us a lot of good advice and everything he had told us so far had been accurate. He asked us repeatedly not to betray him, so that made us think he was telling the truth and we began to trust him.

Next, the secret police began taking Polish men from the labor camp. Sergeant Czeslof said, "Boys, this is bad. Now they are after you. Here's my advice. I know they don't have a list of your names. When they come, if they can't find you, you'll be safe. You can hide up on the factory roof, and I'll just tell them that your squad has already marched out to work. You can lie flat up there, close to the chimney so you have some support and something to hang onto." We tried it the next morning. About ten of us clambered up onto the second story roof and lay as flat as we could, and we got away with it. The secret police came and asked where we were. Sergeant Czeslof told them we were in the working brigade. The police took some other boys. We did it again the next day, and it worked a second time. The next day, Sergeant Czeslof told us, "A *Pułkownik* (Colonel) in the NKVD will be coming tomorrow. He'll interview all the Polish boys who are still here in the yard. He'll assign you a place somewhere in the army. He'll ask you where you want to go from here and it's up to you to think of something you think he'll believe."

We discussed what we should tell the *Pułkownik*. One of the boys had heard that a tank division had recently been in Pomerania, so we agreed that the boys from Pomerania would ask to be posted to the tanks, while those of us from Poznan would request the cavalry. We told Sergeant Czeslof our thoughts. He said, "That sounds like a good enough plan. I'll be damned glad to get you off my hands, because I'm really scared you won't get out of here alive." We agreed among ourselves that none of us had any future in Poland. We all planned to escape to the west, some of us to Germany, some through Czechoslovakia to Austria. I heard in later years that the six boys from my squad who tried to escape through Czechoslovakia were all captured and executed.

The next morning, the boys said to me, "You go first, Jurkowski. If you're lucky, just look over at us and wink and keep going. If it works for you, we'll try the same thing."

I went up to the *Pułkownik* and saluted. He asked me where I was from and where I wanted to go. I told him I was from the Poznan district and wanted to join the cavalry there. He said, "Of course, of course. Very well, here is your certificate with my name and seal on it. Go to the supply office. They will give you food for three days. Go visit your family for three weeks and have a little vacation. After three weeks, report back to the army office here in Lodz."

I said, "Yes, sir," and walked away with that certificate. I couldn't understand why he was letting me go, and my legs were shaking so badly I could hardly walk. The boys were all looking at me and I winked at them. Every one of us was lucky, because that *Pułkownik* knew absolutely nothing. There was no more a cavalry division in Poznan than there was a tank division in Pomerania.

I went home to Krobia and told my brother Wojciech what had happened to me at the officer training school and the labor camp. He said, "I'm not surprised to hear you didn't become an officer. The secret police searched our house twice while you were gone, and they've been sniffing all around the farm."

Wojciech then told me the government was requiring everyone over the age of seventeen to register with the military, and to carry their papers on them at all times. Anyone caught on the street without papers was taken to the investigation office and that was the last they were heard of. He said, "You've brought trouble back here with you. You have several marks against your record now. We'll have to send you someplace where they won't find you."

I lay low at home for a few days while Wojciech contacted various people he thought might be able to help me. Some of his contacts were people who had been active in the resistance during the war. These men were strong Polish nationalists whom the Communists were trying to wipe out as they consolidated their control of Poland. The resistance members still had a network concealing and protecting one another.

Wojciech contacted a man who had been an officer in the resistance and who was now helping people escape. I changed my name so that my family wouldn't get into trouble if the authorities caught me, and I started my journey to the West.

13. Escape from Poland

My resistance contact was a man named Biszek. He ran a small café in the village of Barlinek, about a hundred miles from the East German border. Biszek said I could work in his café kitchen until he could get me across the border. He told me he was already hiding a man who had been a militia commander in the resistance. Biszek and this man had spent the war years executing Gestapo officers who had displayed wanton cruelty. They had worked in secret, wearing Gestapo uniforms. When they found a target, they would say to him, "Absolute silence or we'll kill you." Then they gave the officer a slip listing his crimes and announced that he was condemned to death for his appalling acts. The Gestapo officer would beg for his life and say that he had only obeyed his orders. The commandos would say, "That's right, and we have our orders too," then shoot him with silenced guns. They carried any money and useful equipment away with them, and then they planned their next hit. They spent five years doing this dirty work. Biszek said he told me this story only because he knew my brother and I had been working for the Resistance, and he knew I would keep my mouth shut.

In addition to the militia commander, Biszek employed two German women from Berlin. They had been working at the café since before the war, and once the war started they just stayed put. The three of us enjoyed chatting together in German, and they rather liked me, especially Margaret, the younger one. As the Communists began to squeeze Poland more tightly, the women decided to move back to Berlin. When we said goodbye, Margaret gave me her address, and said, "Andreas, if you ever get to Berlin, please come and see me. Your people have been very kind to us and my family would be glad to help you out."

In November of 1945, after I'd worked at Biszek's café for about three months, the police came with an order stating that everyone had to report to the military, no exceptions. Biszek said, "Andrzej, you need to get to the West. We've already smuggled some people out and we're going to try and ship some more. You can be part of the next group." I was willing to take any chance to get away from the Communists, who were clearly intent on the complete domination of Poland.

Biszek explained their system. "We have a railroad man cooperating with us. The coal car right behind the locomotive has a little secret compartment where three of you can fit. They'll load the coal on top of you. You can get across the border that way. But remember, it's already November, and it's cold as all hell. You may not get as far as West Germany, but you'll certainly get to Berlin if you don't freeze on the way."

I replied, "Thank you for everything you've done. I have family and friends in Berlin, so that's good enough." I packed a small satchel with underwear, a second shirt, and socks. That was all I took, along with my jacket and cap. When I was a boy, I had listened to my uncles tell stories about their hard road home after fighting for Kaiser Wilhelm in World War I. They had walked from a French prisoner of war camp all the way back to Krobia, so I knew enough to travel lightly.

Mother came to Barlinek to bless me and see me off. She gave me her rosary, which I have to this day. She also gave me her gold engagement ring and a fine silver pocket knife. Mother knew the Russians loved silver, and she could tell I liked that knife, too. She said, "Look, your life is more important than these things. Take them and buy your way out. It won't be easy. I'll be praying for you." We both cried when she climbed onto the train back to Krobia.

The day came for my attempt to cross the border. Biszek and the militia commander took me and another hopeful escapee to the switchyard to meet the railroad man. After exchanging greetings, he said, "I have bad news. We arrived here last night from farther east. Somebody must have informed the police that fugitives were on board. They stopped the train, pulled me and the crew off, and then sprayed everything with machine guns. Look at all the bullet holes! It's a good thing that no one was hidden in the secret compartment. I just want you to know what happened. It might happen again, so you need to make up your own mind about what you want to do. I can get you into a passenger car. If you can get across the border into East Germany at Frankfurt an der Oder, you will be out of Communist Poland. You might be able to wiggle through if you have a plausible story and something you can bribe the border guards with. They are still letting people cross from Poland into Germany."

The militia commander looked at me and said, "Look how skinny and pale you are. You have almost no blood left! I think you need to go to Berlin for an urgent intestinal operation that can't be done here in Poland."

That sounded like a good story to me. The railroad man laughed, and said, "That sounds like everybody these days! Okay, you can get on the train this afternoon."

The militia commander produced some official forms and stamps and he wrote out a travel pass for me. Then he asked, "Do you have any German money? They will ask to see it, and you'll need proof that you're prepared to pay for your operation." My face dropped because of course I didn't have any German money. The commando handed me a large sum and I was all set. It troubled me that it was probably money he'd stolen from men he'd killed, but I needed it for my escape, so I took it.

The train was packed with people hoping to move to Germany. Instead of the usual six passengers, there were at least twelve or fourteen people crammed inside the compartment. We chatted nervously as the train chugged towards the border. I could tell that I spoke better German than most of the other passengers. That was the only thing that gave me any confidence at all. I was going into the unknown and I was all alone. I was scared to death. Again, I blessed the memory of my grandfather for encouraging me to become fluent in German. I also spared some thanks for Stöver, since I'd learned a good Berlin accent by working for him.

The train stopped just before the bridge across the Oder River at the border between Poland and Germany. I looked out the window to see squads of military and police officers waiting for us. Some were Poles; some were Russians. They swarmed onto the train like lice and one entered every compartment. A Russian political officer entered ours and asked for everyone's papers. He checked everyone else's, then he read mine. He took a hard look at the stamp from the militia man and asked for my passport. I said, "I don't have one. All I have are these papers, and the doctor told me—"

He interrupted me, asking, "Why are you going to Berlin?"

I replied, "It's for an operation. I have internal lesions. My intestines are infected, and they have to operate right away." I showed him the German money in my wallet.

The officer said, "What else do you have with you?"

I said, "Well, I have this." I showed him the pocket knife that Mother had given me. "It's silver."

He said, "Yeah, I can see it's real silver. What do you want to do with it?"

"I'll give it to you. Please let me go, because I'm very sick. The doctor said I don't have time to wait for a passport. He told me that these papers would let me get across the border and that if I had money I could get the operation immediately."

The Russian said, "Okay, give it to me." Then he turned around and put his hand out behind his back. I put the knife into his paw and he took another look at it to make sure it was the same knife I had showed him. Some previous refugee must have pulled a fast one on him.

I said, "Take it. That's all I have." He grunted, and then turned and left our compartment.

The train whistled, the loudspeaker announced our departure, and we started rolling towards the bridge. Just as the train began moving, a Polish officer came in through the other door of the compartment with his pistol drawn. I said, "We've already had passport control. We had a Russian officer in here just a moment ago."

The Polish officer said, "That doesn't matter, now you'll have a Polish inspection."

I opened the door through which the Russian left. As I turned my back on the Polish officer, I heard the click of his revolver. The Russian officer was still in the corridor, and I cried out to him, "Officer, officer, please come back!" The Russian returned and I said, "Officer, now we're having another passport control, a Polish one."

The Russian looked at the Pole and said, "Get out! I've already checked in here. I told you which compartments I'm checking. What are you doing sneaking along from the back?" The Polish officer jumped out and the Russian locked the compartment door. I was pinned right against the door as we were locked in, but I was grateful to the Russian for coming back, even though I realized he was just protecting his turf from the other parasites.

The Oder river was wide and deep and the bridge had been severely damaged by bombing and shelling. In some places, the arches between the stone piers were so broken that the railroad ties had no bridge framework to support them. The ties were suspended from ropes tied to wooden trusses overhead and the rails lay across those ties. The entire train swayed back and forth as we crawled across the river. My blood froze as I watched the ropes that supported the ties twisting and straining under the weight of the train. The river below us was swift and strong. No one moved, and the compartment was silent except for a couple of people who were praying quietly. Most of the passengers by the windows were looking out. I looked into the middle of the compartment instead, thinking, "Dammit, I don't want to see it if we go in." The people in the middle who couldn't see kept asking, "Are we over?"

The people who were standing by the windows replied, "Oh God, not yet." The train took almost thirty minutes to ease its way across the bridge at no faster than a walking pace. Finally, I could see the locomotive reach the far shore. The engine continued barely creeping. I worried that if one of the supports behind us broke, the weight of the cars would pull the whole train backwards, down into the river. Once the entire train was safely across, we could hear the locomotive chuffing faster as we sped up and away from Poland. Everyone started to talk at once. Some people were crying; some were praying; some were laughing. A chorus of prayers rang out in German and Polish, "*Gott sei dank*" and "*Dzęki Bogu*" (Thanks be to God). I said my own prayers silently to myself, and grinned with relief.

14. Berlin

The train arrived at the Silesia *Bahnhof* in Berlin. I planned to go to my
Aunt Slawa's house in the English sector on the west side of the city, but
I wanted to take a little time to think about everything that had hap-
pened to me, so I went first to the home of my friend Margaret from
Biszek's café.

I knocked on the door and Margaret opened it. She was so surprised and happy to see me that she began to cry. She asked me in and
introduced me to her parents. They were refined and elegant people who
invited me to stay with them for a few days to rest and recover. Margaret's father was an Austrian who worked as a headwaiter in a fancy Berlin restaurant. When I mentioned my aunt on the west side of Berlin,
Margaret's father said, "Travel across the city is still very difficult. The
U-Bahn (subway) is almost destroyed and many of the tunnels are
flooded. Some of the stations are still full of the bodies of people who
were caught in bombing raids. Margaret can take you to your aunt, but
please stay with us for a few days at least." Although they didn't have a
spare bed, Margaret's mother made up a pallet on the floor with cush-
ions and blankets. I slept for two whole days.

On the third morning, Margaret said, "Andreas, I would like you
to accompany me to the main black market," and I realized her family
had no food in their house. I told her I would be happy to use some of
the German money the militia commander had given me. She said, "We
can buy everything there—butter, meat, potatoes. Even molasses. My
parents don't want me to go there alone because trucks full of Russian
soldiers have been coming and grabbing people right off the street. Nobody knows where they are being taken. They don't ever come back." I

was surprised to hear this because the market was in the English-American sector. Margaret told me the Berliners were complaining to the Allies, but the authorities weren't doing anything and the Russians were increasing the frequency of their raids.

The next morning, we went to the open market at the *Tiergarten* and bought red potatoes and some butter. We were still shopping when we heard a loud crash and people yelling, "Here come the Russians!" Panic erupted. The crowd ran deeper into the English-American zone. Margaret dragged me along by my arm because she was afraid I would be captured, and we both knew what would happen if the Russians got hold of me again.

We were lucky and safely made our way back to her apartment. We were visibly upset and her parents knew something had happened. Margaret told them about our narrow escape from the Russian soldiers. Her father cursed at the Allies for not protecting the poor Germans. I thought his reaction was ironic, since it was Germany's own aggression and nationalism that had brought the population to their present misery.

I knew I was a burden on Margaret's family, so the next day I told them I was leaving to stay with Aunt Slawa. They were very gracious and told me repeatedly that if things didn't work out, I was welcome to come back and stay with them. I thanked them for everything they had done for me, and Margaret took me to Slawa's apartment on the west side of Berlin.

*   *   *

When Slawa opened her door, I thought she was going to die of shock and happiness. She screamed and sobbed, "Andrzej! I can't believe it! Is it really you? Come in, come in!" She had received some of the letters we'd sent from Krobia during the war, but she wanted to hear every-thing again from me. Margaret stayed for a while, but she needed to re-turn home before it got dark. Slawa and I talked for hours. Uncle Hans had died of diabetes during the war and Slawa had survived on her own while her two sons were serving in the German military.

We sat in the kitchen as we talked. I could see a gaping hole in the ceiling and a corresponding hole in the floor. The previous winter, a bomb had fallen straight through the building without exploding. The bomb crashed through the roof, passed right through Slawa's tenth floor apartment where we were sitting, and landed in the basement. It was still down there. Many other unexploded bombs were lodged in build-ings all over the city. The residents had to wait their turn for the bomb squad to come disarm them and the people in Slawa's building were still waiting. Although everyone pretended to be blasé, the situation was dangerous.

The first thing I had to tell Slawa was about her niece Jolanta's death. Jolanta was Uncle Stan's daughter, and she and Slawa had always been close. The incident had happened while I was away at officer train-ing school. A Russian officer came into the house and found Jolanta sit-ting in our grandfather's chair. He demanded that she come away with him. She said, "No! You have your own wife in Russia. You just want me to come with you and be your whore." He looked at her, and said, "Either you come with me or I will kill you right here."

Jolanta replied, "Then you will have to kill me." So he did. He pulled out his revolver and shot her in the head, right in our living room. My aunts were there, and they could only watch in horror as she was murdered.

My cousin Jolanta

Poor Slawa. It was hard for me to tell her Jolanta's story. When she had recovered a bit, she told me that my cousin Siegfried would be home from work soon. I was surprised to hear that he was back in Germany. He had been serving in the Germany navy in Saloniki when surrender came. Siegfried saw no reason to stay with the army and be taken prisoner, so he slipped away, put on civilian clothes, walked to a train station, and made his way back to Berlin across eastern Europe. Siegfried's summers on *Dziadzia's* farm in Krobia paid off, because he spoke Polish well enough to conceal that he was German. Of course, Slawa was very happy to have Siegfried home. Slawa's other son, Raimond had been serving the German army on the eastern front and was taken prisoner at the end of the war. He was sent to a Soviet labor camp and held for six years before his release into East Germany, where he died without ever returning to his mother in West Berlin.

Siegfried arrived home and we greeted each other, but his manner seemed reserved. He told me he had resumed working as an architect at his old firm. After we talked for a few minutes, he excused himself and called his mother into the kitchen. I could hear him muttering. He asked her, "Is he here to arrest me? Is he a spy?"

Slawa said, "No, of course not! Wait until you hear all the things he's been through. He's a refugee, not a spy."

When they returned to the room, Siegfried said, "Andreas, I have to be truthful. I thought you wouldn't have come here without a purpose. Russia is supposed to be your ally."

I said, "Whose ally? Stalin isn't my ally. He's not yours, he's not anyone's. Stalin is only for Stalin." I told him about some of my adventures, and he relaxed.

We talked until about 1 a.m. Eventually Siegfried said, "Andreas, it's late and I have to work tomorrow. What are your plans? How can we help?" I told him I planned to head to the West and find some way to make a living there. I reminded him of Uncle Stan's words from before the war—that there would be no future for young people in Poland under the Communists.

Siegfried said, "You got to Berlin just in time, because the Russians are closing the whole border between East and West Germany. I think you still have a few days, but it's getting hard to cross. Here's how it works. Tomorrow, go to the Foreign Bureau. Request an affidavit stating that you need to go to West Germany. Tell them you have relatives there. It's staffed by English and Americans and any excuse will do. They don't investigate anything. Be sure you get all four stamps on the papers: Russian, French, English, and American. And be quick!"

It took me three days to visit all the offices and gather the requisite stamps and permits. On the second evening, Siegfried took me to the opera. The main opera house had been destroyed, so we went to the old opera house near the Silesian station, where we saw a magnificent performance of Tchaikovsky's *Eugene Onegin*. The theater was packed and it was the first time I saw American soldiers. They had sharp-looking uniforms that were well-tailored and crisply ironed.

By the end of the next day, I had collected all the papers and stamps I needed. When Siegfried came home that night, he looked everything over and drew me a map to help me get to the border. The crossing he recommended was at a village somewhat to the east of the city of Uelzen. Siegfried knew a man there who would help me across provided I could pay for it.

By this time, it was late November of 1945 and winter had set in. Travel between Allied-dominated West Germany and Russian-dominated East Germany was still possible, but the Russians were rapidly tightening their control over the border and crossing was becoming difficult. I took the train west from Berlin to the village Siegfried had told me about. The trip was straightforward, but unfortunately everything went wrong after that.

I met Siegfried's contact who told me, "The border here is closed. Just last night, the Russians put up spotlights and you can't get across. They have German Shepherds, and those dogs are keen to catch anyone trying to run across. The guards shoot everyone they see, even if the escapees are already past the border. I'm sorry, but I can't help you here. I hear that the border is still open south of here. Everything there is devastated, and there are a lot more openings where you can slip through."

I had to return to Berlin to find a train that would take me to a different crossing spot. The train carriages were all reserved and refugees like me rode on top of the coal cars. One woman was very kind, and when I climbed up into the coal car, she offered to let me shelter under the blanket she was sharing with two other travelers. We were surprisingly warm even as the falling snow covered us. It seemed almost as if the coal was somehow giving off its own heat. I asked the woman how long she had been traveling on the coal car. She replied that this was her second night.

We rode east through the night back towards Berlin. Russian soldiers stopped the train just before sunrise outside a small station near a ruined village. The soldiers cleared the cars, forcing all the passengers to get off. More soldiers stood on the platform waiting for the passengers and robbing them of their possessions as they stepped out of the carriages. The soldiers grabbed at the luggage and wrestled it away, shooting anyone who resisted. I saw two men shot and a woman dragged away screaming with no one to help her. Despite this, when one of the Russians grabbed my little satchel from me, I chased him down the platform. Fortunately for me, perhaps, he got away. Seeing a German policeman, I went up to tell him what happened. He said, "Well, you won't get it back. Look over past the station, and you can see that there is nothing left here but rubble where our town used to be. It's all just lumps covered with snow. Those soldiers live in holes in the rubble, and they are robbing and living off the proceeds. Don't make a fuss, or they will kill you too." I told him where I was trying to go, and he said that I should simply start walking south and west until I came to the border.

15. Walking to Freedom

As I stood on the station platform deciding on my next move, I talked to a German soldier who was trying to return to his home in western Germany. At the end of the war, his unit had been captured in Poland and loaded onto trains to be sent east to work in Soviet labor camps. This particular man had no control over his bowels, either because of disease or from the extreme hardship and cold he had endured. Instead of killing him, his captors had kicked him off the train and told him to go home. For the first hundred yards, he expected to be shot in the back, but the shot never came. He kept walking until he found a train headed west. When I met him, he'd been riding in coal cars for several days.

I suggested we travel together to try and find an open border crossing. At first the soldier was reluctant to be my companion. He said, "I'm sick and I stink."

I said, "Well, I don't smell so great myself right now and it's only going to get worse."

The German said, "It's worse than that. I have a lot of sins on my head for things I did in the war, and I don't think a Polish man would want to be with me."

I said, "You know, the war is over. You were soldiers. The generals spent the war hiding in Berlin. They bear the guilt, not you. You weren't Gestapo. You weren't *Hitlerjugend*. You will make your peace with God and with other people as you live the rest of your life. It doesn't make any difference to me what you did or how you feel about it. We just have to get along."

Our path led through an area that had been heavily contested. The fields were torn up by bombs and tanks. We had no food, so as we walked along, we looked for vegetables in the frozen fields. We found carrots, potatoes, and rutabagas. We also found the bodies of dead soldiers. Arms and legs stuck out of the ground. We picked up vegetables that were right next to exposed body parts—frozen hands with fingers clawing out of the soil, feet that were naked because the boots had been stolen from the corpses. People who don't know what hunger is might find this distressing, but we wiped the dirt off those vegetables and ate them raw. After a day, my intestines rebelled and then we both had diarrhea. We slept at night in ruined barns and farm buildings, pulling straw together to make little nests to sleep in.

After a week or so of walking, we arrived in a small village just at dusk. Snow was falling heavily, so I asked around for a place to spend the night. A man told us to try a house down the road. I knocked on the door and asked the man who opened it if he knew where we could get a bed for the night.

The man was a German teacher. We spoke for a few minutes and he invited me inside. He introduced me to his wife, and they agreed that I could stay the night. My companion wouldn't come inside. He said, "I am too sick to enter your home." The woman took the soldier to the hospital and came back without him. He was admitted right away and I never saw him again.

The couple said it was fortunate that I had arrived that night, because the next day they planned to meet their daughter at a nearby border crossing and they could show me the way. Their daughter was returning home from a visit to her brother in the English sector. I arose the next morning filled with hope that my journey was almost over. The couple were gracious hosts and they shared their breakfast of tea and toast with jam with me. Then we walked together for about half a mile to the border crossing.

As we came around a corner, I could see trouble. Everything was closed and nobody could cross, neither to the east nor to the west. We could see the daughter standing on the other side of the gates and hear her calling to her parents that she wasn't being allowed to cross. The English guards on the western side said they would let people through — they didn't want to hold anyone back — but the Russians wouldn't let anybody cross in either direction. The girl said to the Russian guards, "But I have all the papers. I got them before I left, and I followed all the regulations so I could visit my brother and then come home." The soldiers told her no and waved her back with their guns. The girl's parents had to go home without her.

After this disappointment, the German teacher told me he knew a man who could help me cross the border at night. He escorted me to the guide, but the man panicked when we met. He said, "I can't help you, because I don't want the responsibility if you get shot. The Soviets have tightened up the border zone here with searchlights and guard dogs. You should head south to the next crossing and see if you can get through there. The Russians said they would open the border there at Christmas so people can visit their families."

I walked south for three more days to another village on the border. This crossing was also closed, although it was supposed to open in a few days for the Christmas holiday. Almost a hundred refugees were sheltering in the barn of a nearby farm. The woman who owned it told me she had room for me if I wanted to stay until the border reopened. She gave me a bundle of straw to sleep in and I camped there in her barn along with everyone else. The woman boiled potatoes for us, although she only had enough for one apiece.

The next morning, the woman told everyone she was out of potatoes. She had heard the border wasn't going to open for a week, but she'd also heard a rumor that Russian soldiers along the border were paying with bread for men to cut wood to heat their barracks. She suggested that several of us go work for the Russians so we could bring back bread for ourselves and to help her feed the other refugees. Her proposal made me uneasy, because I suspected the Russians would simply march me off at gunpoint to a labor camp. Despite my fears, I went with some other men to find the soldiers. They gave us axes and saws to cut trees for firewood. The freezing rain and deep mud made for miserable work and my hopelessness grew as I weakened from malnutrition. I tried to keep *Dziadzia's* old saying in mind, "We're not made of sugar. We won't melt," but it was difficult to stay positive as my situation deteriorated with each new day.

The first day we cut wood was Christmas day. The border did not open. We cut wood every day for the next week. Each night we walked back to the barn and shared the Russian bread. The seventh morning, New Year's Day, 1946, was another cold, wet one. We were on our way back to the woodlot when a Russian officer cantered up to us on a beautiful Arabian horse. He skidded to a stop and his horse slopped mud all over us. The officer thought this was funny and laughed at our wet and filthy state. Then he said, "Okay, line up behind me, you are marching now." My heart sank into my shoes. I thought to myself, "All this struggle and terror and the Russians have me after all."

He said, "Does everyone here want to cross the border?"

Oh, my God, yes, we did!

"Okay, march!"

The Russian officer marched us about a mile to the border. There was a line of several hundred people waiting to cross. Many pushed bicycles laden with all their belongings, while others dragged handcarts or carried suitcases. They were Poles, people from the Baltic states, and East Berliners. The line moved slowly as Russian guards checked everyone's papers. I was still carrying mine from the Foreign Bureau in Berlin. When the guard looked at them, I pointed to the Russian stamp, and he said, "Okay, go on."

I walked across the twenty yards that separated the two gates— and there I was in the English zone. I was elated and said some prayers in thanksgiving. Behind me, the line had become undisciplined. Russian soldiers were grabbing luggage, and the refugees were fighting back. Shots were fired. People were screaming and running. A British officer ran out from the guard house and fired his pistol in the air repeatedly until order was restored. He ordered the Russian soldiers to keep away from people crossing the border. Surprisingly, the soldiers listened to him and backed off. I put the border behind me and turned my face to the west.

16. Working for the U.S. Army

I was in West Germany! I wasn't completely alone though, because I was covered in lice. Oh lord, they were in my hair, in my socks, and all over my body. The worst part was when they went into my ears. The English administrators knew how to handle lice. All of the refugees were sent to a hall for delousing. We stripped and had DDT poured over us and over our clothing. We shook out our clothes, put them back on, washed our hands and faces, and climbed aboard buses to be taken to a military installation in the town of Fallingbostel. Barracks there had been part of a P.O.W. camp during the war. Now they were being used to house displaced persons from all over Europe.

The British army fed me, gave me a bed in the barracks, and registered me as a displaced person. I felt good because I could use my real name again. I had been using a false name since the start of my journey, since there was real danger of retribution to my family if the Communist authorities found out I had escaped to the west. I worried that my family might be punished for receiving mail from the west, so I sent a letter to Aunt Slawa in West Berlin and she let my mother know that I had made it to the English sector.

I spoke no English when I arrived, but I tried to learn from anyone who would talk to me and I began picking it up quickly. I was fortunate because I had started learning other languages from an early age and that made it relatively easy for me to learn English.

After I had rested in the barracks for a few days, someone told me that the U.S. Army was hiring Poles to serve as guards to replace homeward-bound American soldiers. The Army was also in need of interpreters. Hearing this, I took a train to the recruiting office in Munich, where

I told a sergeant my war history. "Look, this is where I worked during the war. When the war was over, I tried to join the Polish army. It was controlled by the NKVD and they wouldn't accept me. I knew that I wouldn't have any kind of life under the Communists. I took off for the west and here I am."

The U.S. Army was happy to hire me because I knew Polish, German, and Russian, and my English was coming along. The sergeant directed me to enlist in the Polish Guard, a paramilitary organization employed by the U.S. Army to provide security services. Then I was sent to a U.S. Army base at Giessen, north of Frankfurt.

My boss was Major Lewis. He was a big, jolly man from California. I am six feet tall, but he was even taller, and much heavier. He was so big that the whole room shook when he laughed. His work was serious, though. His office oversaw criminal investigations and the questioning and prosecuting of offenders. Major Lewis put me to work taking notes while prisoners were being interrogated. I stayed silent during the interviews. The prisoners didn't know which languages I understood. Sometimes when the officers left the room, the prisoners talked among themselves, and I would record and translate what they said.

I never sat in on the interrogation of any spies or master criminals. In general, our office dealt with petty criminals, such as people who had been caught stealing. Sometimes we prosecuted sexual assault cases. Things were very tough in Germany. Food was rationed and people could no longer get coffee, chocolate, cigarettes, or other little luxuries. I was surprised at how many American soldiers were involved in the black market, stealing goods from American depots and selling to the

Germans. One of the most popular items was American crackers — people in Germany had never seen them before, and they were in great demand.

In my experience, if you need to know something important, it is a bad idea to depend exclusively on translators. The newspapermen seemed to believe anything the translators told them. Sometimes reporters were fed outrageous stories, and they published them. Someone who doesn't know or can't learn the language where he or she is working shouldn't be working there. Major Lewis often told me that he valued my language skills and discretion.

*   *   *

Not long after I joined the Polish Guard, Stalin objected to the employment of Eastern European refugees by American forces. He argued that we should be sent back to rebuild our war-torn countries. I thought, right, he wants to use us for fertilizer, nothing more. Stalin told Truman that contractors shouldn't be allowed to wear official military uniforms. Truman agreed with Stalin that non-American contractors should be distinguishable from the regular army, so our Polish Guard uniforms were all dyed navy blue.

I was at work one morning when Major Lewis came into the office with an intelligence signal saying a Soviet commission would be inspecting the troops in the American zone, as was their right under the treaties that ended the war. The inspection was scheduled for the following day. The signal also said that the Soviets intended to kidnap any Polish soldiers who were working for the Americans, and that they would be able to identify us by our distinctive blue uniforms. They planned to ambush us as we marched along a short street called the Kutsgasse that lay between our barracks and the office. The Soviets planned to block both ends of the street and force us into trucks at gunpoint.

The next morning, our officers drew their revolvers as we entered the Kutsgasse. We soldiers picked up cobblestones and sheltered in the doorways of the apartment buildings. A small war broke out when Soviet trucks blocked the ends of the street. Our officers shot at the trucks and we pelted the troops with stones. The Soviet troops retreated in confusion and left us to march to work. Later, Major Lewis told us with a wink that our attack on the poor defenseless Soviet troops had become an international incident and that Mrs. Roosevelt was very upset with us, but we never heard any more about it.

When I arrived in Giessen, I met a Polish officer named Ludwig Kraski. He had been captured early in the war and spent six years in a military prison camp in western Germany. After his release, he heard the Americans were employing Eastern European contractors, so he enlisted in the Polish Guard, was given the rank of Captain, and put in charge of a company of Polish soldiers. Captain Kraski and his wife Olenka became my close friends.

After I began working for Major Lewis, the Army Counter Intelligence Corps (CIC) officer assigned someone to follow me wherever I went. I spotted my "tail" right away and recognized him as a man named Captain Jacobson. Everyone knew who he was and we all wondered about him, because he never seemed to have any actual duties. After a month or two of seeing Captain Jacobson everywhere I went, I complained to Captain Kraski, who talked to Major Lewis for me. Major Lewis said, "Dammit, I am going to fix this once and for all. Andrew, the next time you see Captain Jacobson behind you, you turn around and tell him nicely, 'Captain Jacobson, please quit spying on me.' Then he will have to report to me that you have approached him and I can tell him to cut out this bullshit." I spoke to Captain Jacobson and the poor guy was embarrassed. He hadn't realized that I knew he was following me.

Captain Kraski told Major Lewis he was not doing a good job of looking for spies. He said, "You are surrounded by spies and you don't have a clue. You have the CIC following that Polish kid who has told the truth about everything he's been through, while you're surrounded by bad guys you don't even know about." Major Lewis took Captain Kraski's lecture seriously and sent the chief CIA officer, Tony Mark, to interview him. Mark was American born. His original name was Markuczewicz, although he changed it to Mark when he joined the CIA. He spoke excellent German, French, Polish, and English. The CIA were looking for a group of organized criminals that was operating in the area. After Captain Kraski gave him some tips, Mark and his team planned a sting operation and were able to arrest the gang.

I worked for Major Lewis from the start of 1946 through 1948. Our unit was stationed in Giessen for the first eighteen months. After this, our group was transferred because Soviet agents were continually approaching Polish soldiers. They tried to blackmail us into working as spies by threatening our families back home. The Americans moved our unit to the smaller town of Rodheim, where it would be harder for the Soviet agents to remain covert.

*   *   *

My friend Captain Kraski and his wife Olenka had no children of their own, so they appreciated my company and all but adopted me during the two years we spent together. Like her husband, Olenka Kraski was well-educated. She was from a noble Polish family that had lived in Vienna before the war. One of her aunts had been the Mother Superior of a religious order in western Poland; her portrait is still displayed in the Poznan historical museum. *Pani* Olenka spoke excellent English and she had studied American literature in secondary school. She especially enjoyed the writings of John Steinbeck. This gave her topics to discuss with the American military wives who had joined their husbands in Rodheim. *Pani* Olenka and Mrs. Lewis became particularly good friends and together they organized many social occasions that were aimed at fostering positive relationships between the Polish and American forces and their families.

One evening, Mrs. Lewis organized a formal reception for the wives of the American officers. All the Polish officers wore their dress uniforms. They carried swords and wore boots that came up higher than their knees, and they each carried a bouquet of roses. As each lady entered the ballroom, she was announced, saluted, and presented with a bouquet. The heel-clicking and hand-kissing went on all night and the officers' dashing elegance overwhelmed the American ladies.

Mrs. Lewis arranged for Dr. Taran and his daughter to provide piano entertainment for the evening. Dr. Taran was a concert pianist as well as a medical doctor. He was a White Russian who had fled to Poland after the Russian revolution to become a citizen and an officer in the Polish army. Like Captain Kraski, he had spent six years as a prisoner of war in a camp in western Germany. He got his wife and daughter out of Poland at the end of the war and they joined him in Giessen.

One of the guests was Mrs. LaSalle. Before the war, her husband, Captain LaSalle, had been a big shot in the Detroit city government. Mrs. LaSalle was accustomed to living among the wealthy and cultivated people of high society. She adored classical music, especially Chopin. When Dr. Taran began his performance with a Chopin sonata, Mrs. LaSalle was overcome with almost hysterical rapture. She sobbed and moaned so loudly the Doctor thought she was having a seizure and interrupted his playing to ask if she needed help. Captain LaSalle tried to hush her, but Mrs. LaSalle couldn't stop exclaiming about her beloved Chopin. The audience was uncomfortable at first, but when they realized how much pleasure Mrs. LaSalle was taking in the music, everyone relaxed, and the evening was ultimately a great success.

*   *   *

Captain Kraski was Lutheran while *Pani* Olenka was Catholic. They were open-minded about religion and we had many philosophical discussions. Captain Kraski had met the Lutheran pastor Dietrich Bonhoeffer when they were locked up in the same military prison camp during the war. As a boy, I had been taught that when I passed a Catholic church I should take off my hat out of respect. Captain Kraski once asked me, "Andrzej, I have a question that's been bothering me for a while. Why do you only take your hat off when you pass a Catholic church, but not when you pass a Protestant church?"

I said, "Well, the Catholic church is my church."

He lectured me, "Look here, young man. Don't do this to yourself. Don't you think it's the same God in both churches? There are many different expressions and different philosophies of God's love. You should have respect for all of them. How could merciful God want to kill people? My pastor Dietrich was punished for not renouncing God, and I respect his teaching."

Captain Kraski's speech reminded me of my grandfather, *Dziadzia* Walenty. I had heard him express the same idea many times — we show our love for God by helping one another and all religions are worthy of respect. *Dziadzia* passed his philosophy of tolerance and generosity to me and it has stayed with me all my life.

I thought my English had become quite good, but Captain Kraski felt I needed more formal instruction. He sent me to a woman named *Frau* Hupt for lessons. She was an excellent teacher who spoke with a proper British accent. That accent almost broke my tongue, but I mastered it. In fact, after I emigrated to America and started working in an auto plant, my co-workers thought I was English instead of Polish and called me "Limey." After two years of lessons, *Frau* Hupt told Captain Kraski that she had nothing more to teach me. She thought my English was fine, and my German outstanding.

Through the Kraskis, I became friends with *Frau Doktor* Geil. She and her husband lived in a beautiful lakefront home on the outskirts of Rodheim, and they hosted many memorable parties. I enjoyed being around her, because she always defended me to Captain Kraski, saying, "I don't see anything wrong with Andrew's English and German. He speaks beautifully and he has very nice manners." *Frau Doktor* Geil was from a noble Polish family and had grown up on the family estate near Wilna, in Lithuania. She married a German pharmaceutical chemist, and they had spent the war in Rodheim. I found their beautiful daughter Irina quite attractive, although she was very independent and didn't want to go out with me.

Frau Doktor Geil's husband had joined the Nazi party in an attempt to shield their son from military service by getting permission to send him to Switzerland for college. The boy was drafted anyway and told his mother, "Well, I hope I get posted to Wilna, because I had such lovely times visiting my grandparents there every summer when I was a child." Indeed, he was sent to Wilna and was killed there fighting on the eastern front.

Frau Doktor Geil was able to go to Wilna to recover her son's body and have him buried in the family churchyard. After his death, she spent the war helping people who had escaped from the Gestapo or prison camps. She told her husband if he denounced her, she'd betray him to the secret police. But she told me, "You know what? It wasn't true—I wouldn't have denounced him. I was just threatening him because I knew I had to do something to help people."

*   *   *

Once, when I was travelling on the express train from Giessen to Munich, the ticket collector came through and I recognized him as *Herr* Hause, Stöver's assistant, who had been sent from Pudliszki to the eastern front. I gasped and cried, "*Herr* Hause, is it really you?" The man blanched and wouldn't look at me. He turned and hurried out of the car without speaking. A different ticket collector came in after that. I don't know why *Herr* Hause was afraid to meet me. He had never harmed me or my family. Perhaps he had a guilty conscience and couldn't remember if he had injured me or not.

Another time, when I was taking the streetcar in Giessen, a young woman entered the car and I thought to myself, "My God, that's Adelheide Gross! How did she get here from Berlin?" She had been *Herr*

Stöver's secretary back at Pudliszki. I tipped my cap as I got off the streetcar, although I didn't speak to her.

Later that day, a young woman came to the barracks and asked for me at the guard post. I wasn't there, but when I returned the guard grinned at me and said, "Oh, you big stud, you had such a pretty girl asking for you."

I asked him if she'd left a name and he replied, "*Fraulein* Adelheide Gross. She said she recognized you on the streetcar." It turned out that Adelheide Gross was friends with *Frau Doktor* Geil. Adelheide and I spent a lot of time together that summer going dancing and visiting the park along the river.

I made other friends during my service in Giessen and Rodheim. Alfons Klink was another member of the Polish Guard who came from near Poznan, where he had been a printer at the famous St. Adalbert publishing company. Alfons was captured early in the war and spent the next six years working on a German farm. The farm owner was serving in the German army and his wife kept busy in his absence trying to seduce the prisoners. The penalty for getting caught with her was death, so Alfons resisted her advances, although several other prisoners surrendered to her charms and paid the price. Alfons's wife, Tereska Grabowska, had also come from Poznan. The Nazis compelled many young Polish women to work as *Dienstmädchen* (housemaids), although this was a euphemism, since many of the women were forced to prostitute themselves to the German officers. Tereska's mother managed to get her daughter a job working as a nanny for a noble family in Luxemburg, and she spent the war in safety.

*   *   *

After a year in the U.S. Army, I had gained a little weight, so I decided to purchase a much-needed civilian suit. Clothing was still rationed, but I had saved my coupons and traded chocolate and cigarettes for more. I was talking about this in the office and one of my colleagues introduced me to a man who told me he would take me to Siegelsdorf. This was a village near Frankfurt where there were many tailor shops. During the war, it had been a resort area for Nazi party officials. After the war, the town was almost deserted until the occupying government turned it into a settlement for Jewish refugees. They formed a *yiddische Geschäft*, a Jewish business village, with many tailors and haberdashers.

My guide and I took the train from Rodheim to Siegelsdorf and walked from the station to the main street. A man recognized my companion and came up to us. He said, "Oh, come in, come in, I have a little shop, and I can tailor you a fine suit."

My companion said, "Oh, I know this guy — he's good. Let's look in his shop." The next thing I knew, I was being measured for a suit and dress shirts, and choosing a couple of silk ties. It turned out that my guide was colluding with the tailor and had taken me to him in exchange for a finder's fee. I never got to look in any of the other shops. Fortunately, I knew how to pick a quality fabric and the suit was well made, so things worked out.

*   *   *

After two years, Captain Kraski and his wife received U.S. passports and permission to emigrate to America. *Frau* Heinz, the Kraski's German landlady, held a goodbye party for them. I was helping in the kitchen when her maid had a sudden religious fit. She ranted about how the German people were doomed to burn in hell because of the evil they had done in the war. The Germans were incarnations of the devil himself because they weren't Catholic and didn't believe in the true God. She was hysterical with hatred and malice, especially towards non-Catholics. I tried to tell her that God loved Protestants and Jews too, and we eventually got her calmed down so the party could begin.

I was introduced to the host, *Herr Doktor* Heinz, who was a specialist dentist-physician. I greeted him with respect and said I was honored to make his acquaintance. He looked at me and called to his wife, "Ani, did you hear this? This Polish soldier is honored to meet me. That's impossible."

Frau Heinz said, "Why would you be surprised? Andreas is polite, he has nice manners, and of course he greeted you respectfully."

Herr Doktor Heinz replied, "Yes, but we are enemies."

I looked him in the eye, and said, "*Herr Doktor*, I am not your enemy. That was the past and it is over. I will not live with hatred in my heart. What happened, happened. I don't know if you have any guilt, or if you did anything you are ashamed of, but the war is over."

Herr Doktor Heinz said, "No, I did nothing wrong, but I knew what was happening and I am ashamed. I am surprised that you want to be in our company. I respect your greeting, and the same to you."

*   *   *

When I had saved up some leave, I took a trip to Bavaria to visit Hitler's alpine vacation retreat at Berchtesgaden. In those days, tourists arranged to rent rooms in private homes rather than staying at hotels, so when I arrived by train, I began to look for a room. I met a man with a room to rent and said, "*Guten Morgen.*" He glared at me and said, "You must be Prussian."

I replied, "No, I am Polish."

He insisted, "No, I am sure you are Prussian." I offered to show him my identity papers. He said, "All these people from the east are not Germans; they are Prussians. The Bavarians are the only true Germans and Bavaria is the heart of Germany."

I answered, "I didn't know that. Thank you for teaching me something new about geography and history."

He said, "You need to learn how to greet people properly. Here we say "*Grüss Gott*, Praise to God. There is no *Guten Morgen* here."

I replied, "Thank you. Now that I know how you feel, I will do that." I guess that was polite enough for him, because then he rented me a room. Our interaction led me to reflect on how people's tribal natures contributed to wars. Even after all the horrors we had passed through, this man was focused on defining himself and his own small tribe as the only true Germans, and everyone else as other, lesser beings.

I spent several days in and around Berchtesgaden, mostly hiking in the woods. My room overlooked a monastery of cloistered monks. My host told me he had watched the monks try to protect Jews, refugees, and people from the resistance. The Gestapo came and beat the monks to force them to admit what they were doing. He said Bavarians couldn't forgive Hitler for his deeds against the monks. I thought to myself that Hitler had surely done many more unforgiveable things and this man was still focused only on his own small tribe. At the same time, I realized that anything that might help people see others as equally human might lead to better understanding and fewer wars.

Andrew visiting Frankfurt, 1947

17. My Family's Life in Communist Poland

Tina in Bielsko-Biala with her fur collar and muff, 1949

After the war ended, my brother, Wojciech, found work as a bookkeeper in the city of Bielsko-Biała. This is a famous textile manufacturing center in a mountainous area about fifty miles west of Krakow, not far from Poland's border with Czechoslovakia. The surrounding region is famous for the production of high quality wool. The pure waters of the Bielsko river are excellent for processing wool into fine fabric, and the river itself powers the spinning and weaving machinery. Wojciech managed to find jobs for our sisters, Tina and Maria, so they could live together with Mother and Tina's little girl in an apartment in Bielsko.

Tina worked as an accountant for the same textile factory that employed Wojciech. Soon after she arrived, her supervisor tried to get her to defraud the company by diverting a little of the income into a special account. Tina refused, saying, "Why would you ask me to do that? I'd be taking all the risk while you'd get all the money. The inspectors would catch me, not you, and I won't go to jail for anybody!"

Tina told Wojciech about this incident. He sighed and said, "I already covered up for him once when he tried his skimming tricks. Now he's going to try to get you fired." Wojciech arranged for Tina to transfer to a different office in Bielsko-Biała, where a cousin of our grandmother worked. This cousin was *Pan* Bizkupski, an older man we had not met before. He was very helpful in finding work for Tina and Maria. During the war, the Gestapo had kidnapped his beautiful blonde daughter, Wanda. Many Polish women of the "Aryan type" were taken to breed babies for Hitler. Wanda committed suicide by jumping from a cliff rather than submit to that fate.

While Tina worked in an office, our sister Maria and her friend Nusia worked as sales clerks in a retail fabric shop. Almost all consumer goods, including food and clothing, were rationed in the post-war years. Communist Party members were issued a special I.D. along with coupons that permitted them to shop for higher quality merchandise. Some Poles joined the Party solely to get exclusive shopping privileges. Most of the shop's customers were Party members, although the shop also sold to regular Poles if they had ration coupons. Regular citizens learned to wear their oldest clothing when they applied for a clothing permit, because without a demonstration of need, their request would be denied.

Every part of the Polish economy was entangled in the black market. Dishonesty was the way of life because it was the only way for ordinary people to get by. The head of the fabric shop had connections with the secret police. The shop had a special room behind a green curtain for the restricted merchandise. When party members came in, the owner would wait on them himself in the back room. Maria and Nusia could hear cloth being measured and cut and money changing hands, but the transactions never went into the ledger.

Everyone skimmed what they could and bartered for necessities. When Party members ordered goods like coffee or sugar, the clerk would put a finger on the scale to give a short weight and then sell or trade the surplus on the black market. Maria and Nusia did this too. Every time they measured fabric for a customer, they wrote in the ledger that they had sold a few more inches than they really had, so there might be a yard or two of extra fabric left on the end of each bolt that they could take home and use for barter.

Maria and Nusia concealed the extra fabric and smuggled it home under their clothes. A Jewish merchant from Bielsko named Bernard Schweidt lived in an apartment across the plaza. He was a middle-man who traded fabric on the black market and he paid Maria and Nusia for any cloth they could smuggle out of their shop. He and Maria became good friends.

Bernard had grown up in a family of shopkeepers in Bielsko, and when I met him years later in America, he gave me some advice about salesmanship that he'd heard from his father. Bernard made sure he sold something to the first customer who came into his shop on a Monday morning, even if it was at a loss. He said it brought luck for the rest of the week, and in bad times, customers would remember that he was always ready to make a deal. Bernard was always very successful and he had a reputation for fairness. He once told me he thought the Jews had been too arrogant towards the Poles. Just before the war, some Jews had a saying that the world was like a barrel. They said, "We Jews are on the bottom, the Poles are in the middle, the Germans are on the top. After this war ends, the barrel will flip over, and we Jews will be on top, the Germans will be on the bottom, and you Poles will still be in the middle." It seemed as if the Jews felt the Poles were inconsequential because we were just peasant farmers, while the Jews were more important and sophisticated because they owned all the buildings and had all the money.

Bernard had been a peddler before the war. He and his partner, another Jew, supplied fabric from Bielsko to shops in villages across Russia. They walked from town to town pulling a sled with their goods. They traveled mostly at night so they would encounter fewer of the police patrols who demanded bribes to let them pass. Bernard's partner was a nervous fellow who panicked when he heard wolves howling. One night, when they had to pull the sled over a steep pass, Bernard said, "I hear the wolves! Let's hurry!" His partner abandoned Bernard and the sled, and ran all the way to the next village. Bernard yelled, "Wait! I was joking, come back," but the guy never stopped, and Bernard had to pull the sled over the pass all by himself.

Bernard and his partner survived the early years of the war by travelling deep into Siberia, but even there they couldn't elude Stalin's grasp. In 1944, they were arrested and conscripted into the Soviet Army. The men were compelled at gunpoint to serve as human mine sweepers. They marched in front of the Soviet troops who were pursuing the Germans as they retreated from Leningrad. Only twelve men survived from Bernard's unit of fifty, and Bernard himself was wounded multiple times. I have never seen a man with so many scars.

Bernard and his partner both returned to Bielsko-Biała after the war. Neither of them had any family left. Bernard's former associates invited him to join the secret police and collaborate with the Communists controlling Poland. A lot of money could be made from selling merchandise on the black market and taking bribes, but Bernard refused to join. He said, "I am Jewish and I am Polish. I will never betray my own people to the secret police, neither the Jews nor the Poles." He worried his associates would denounce him for black market dealing and get him thrown into prison, but he avoided trouble by paying off Party officials. The whole system was as corrupt as hell, with denunciation and bribery a way of life.

*   *   *

One evening, Maria didn't come home from work. Someone had tipped off the police that she occasionally carried black market merchandise. She didn't have any illicit goods on her that night, but she was arrested, taken downtown, and thrown into jail. As the evening got late, Tina finally said, "Mother, something must be wrong. I'd better go to the police station and ask if they've seen Maria."

At the station, the holding cell faced the main entrance, so a visitor could see from the front door who was in jail. When Tina rang the bell, the door opened, and she saw Maria in the holding cell. Maria yelled, "Tina, go home! Get away!"

Tina had just turned around to leave when an officer came out and asked why she had rung the bell. She replied, "Because I'm looking for my sister and I can see she's been arrested."

The officer said, "What's her name?"

Tina answered, "Maria Jurkowska. Why is she here?"

The officer replied only, "She's under suspicion.

Tina went home and warned everyone to prepare for a police raid. Mother gathered all the family's black market goods and prepared to burn them. One of their neighbors was a woman of French descent whose husband was the police informer for the building. At that time, every apartment building had a paid Party agent who kept track of foreign visitors, black market dealings, and political talk. The French woman was always angry with her husband because he didn't have a proper job. He just hung around on street corners, gossiping and getting paid for denouncing his fellow Poles.

When Tina told the French woman that Maria had been arrested, and that everyone needed to destroy their illicit goods, the woman offered to conceal their things because she knew the police wouldn't search her apartment. The French woman was always very supportive of her neighbors, who were regular Poles just trying to scrape by under the corrupt Communist system.

Tina took some things to the French woman's apartment and was astonished to overhear her scolding her husband for being a traitor and a lazy bum. The woman said, "Without the black market, our family would have nothing to eat, because you don't work enough to qualify for ration stamps. And you're too lazy to stand in the long lines at the grocery stores like *Pani* Jurkowska does. I'm not afraid of you and if you try to report me, I'll tell the police all kinds of things about you."

The French woman worked in a meat processing factory that made canned hams. These were exported all over the world, yet not a single ham was ever sold to a Polish citizen who wasn't a Party member. The French woman would cut off pieces of meat and hide them under her clothing to bring home and serve to her family. She dared her husband to denounce her, but he never did, because he knew they would starve without her.

The police interrogated Maria all night, but they had no evidence and she was allowed to return home. Meanwhile, the police arrived to search the apartment. When they saw Tina standing at the entrance, they realized she had already alerted the residents, so they cancelled the raid.

When they lived in Bielsko-Biała, Mother and my sisters befriended two women, *Pani* Ola and her mother. Their family had owned a manor in eastern Poland but they lost it when the Russians invaded at the start of the war. The father of the family took a job working on the railroad because he thought it might help his family escape. Unfortunately, instead of working on routes that ran towards the West, he was put to work on the Trans-Siberian railroad, and spent several years running back and forth from Lvov into deepest Siberia. Eventually the father was drafted, as were *Pani* Ola and her brother. All three of them fought with the Soviet Army at Stalingrad. *Pani* Ola survived, but her father and brother were both killed. After the war, *Pani* Ola returned to Bielsko-Biała where her mother had lived during the war. They raised vegetables and rabbits on their small farm. The two women pulled a little hand cart to town so they could sell their produce at the weekly market. Mother worked out a scheme to meet the women on the way to market and buy what she wanted from their little cart before they got into town. That way, the women didn't have to pay the market fee, while Mother got a deal on the vegetables. Poor *Pani* Ola had been crippled during the war and then she developed tuberculosis. After I got to America, I arranged for TB drugs to be mailed to her and she made a full recovery.

That's how the Polish people lived under the Communists. The authorities knew that everyone depended on the black market. There weren't enough goods in the stores. People stole from their workplaces and bartered with each other just to get by.

PART IV

1949 - 2017

18. Welcome to America

While I was working in Giessen, I met an American girl of Polish descent named Frieda Lebedinski. She was a stenographer working in General Eisenhower's office. Frieda spoke excellent Polish and was a lovely dancer. We enjoyed each other's company for almost a year before she was transferred to a different military base. As we parted, she said, "If you don't have any place to go when you get to the United States, you can come to Detroit and my family will take care of you." I told her I didn't know if I'd ever get to America, but I assured her that if I did, I would certainly come and visit.

Returning home to Poland was not an option for me as long as the Communists were running my country, but I didn't want to stay in Germany either. Like the other displaced people I met, I didn't trust the superficially friendly attitude that most Germans expressed towards us. It seemed an artifact of U.S. occupation rather than a true change in mindset. Most important, we all feared continued Soviet aggression and expansion and wanted to put an ocean between the Soviet Union and wherever we ended up.

I discussed various immigration options with other refugees. Some people planned to go to Canada or Australia, but for several reasons going to the United States appealed most to me. I liked most of the Americans I met while I was working for the U.S. Army. In general, they seemed honest and fair in their dealings, and they told me America offered a lot of opportunity for hard workers. I believed them because my best friends, Captain Kraski and Alfons Klink, both moved to America as soon as they could, and found jobs almost immediately. I hoped that my work for the U.S. Army would give me preferential treatment in applying for an American visa.

Every few months I went to the U.S. Consulate in Frankfurt and applied for a passport so I could emigrate to America, but I never received one. After I'd been working for Major Lewis for almost three years, he asked me why I was always going to Frankfurt. I told him that no matter how many times I applied for a U.S. passport, I was always rejected. Surprised, he asked, "Don't they know you're working for the American Army? Why in hell won't they process your application?" He called the consulate, and then things started to move.

Major Lewis told me I should apply for work as a special services translator. Eventually the consulate sent me a work visa and a contract for employment in the U.S. I was sponsored by a man named Mr. Terry in Winona, Minnesota, through the Catholic Social Services organization. Mr. Terry would pay for my transportation from Frankfurt to Minnesota, give me a job, and help me find a place to live. This would cost him $300 up front, and I would repay him out of my salary. The paperwork said that Mr. Terry ran a big garage for farming equipment, so I thought maybe he needed a translator to help him with importing and exporting.

It seemed like fate was in my favor. In a burst of optimism, I bought the finest camera I could afford, a German Leica. During the occupation, Stöver had been very proud of his fancy camera, and I was happy to acquire one that was as sophisticated as his. Learning to use it was a challenge, but eventually I caught on and took pictures of the area where I was living. I anticipated recording my life in America and sending pictures back to my family.

        *   *   *

I left for America in December, 1948 on the *USS Marine Flasher,* a converted troopship making her final voyage. Most of the passengers were refugees immigrating to the U.S., although some returning troops accompanied us. The winter crossing took ten days and was extremely rough. I was assigned a berth on one of the ship's lowest decks, where our hammocks hung in tiers right up to the ceiling. Almost everyone in my compartment was seasick and the stuffy air made it difficult to breathe. Someone told me the motion was easier the lower you were in the ship, but between the fetid atmosphere and the vigorous pitching and rolling, I was overcome with nausea and couldn't eat for almost the entire crossing. The seas didn't calm until the day before we reached New York harbor. I had finally settled into a restful sleep when a cry echoed down through all the decks that the Statue of Liberty was in view. Of course, all of the passengers, including me, ran to the rail for our first glimpse of America. The sight was inspirational and certainly worth a photograph. Almost as soon as I arrived on deck, I realized I had left my camera in my hammock. Sadly, by the time I made it back down to my berth on the lowest level, the camera was gone. I reported the theft to the purser, who told me one of the crewmen had taken my camera and concealed it in some secret hiding place so he could smuggle it off the ship after the passengers had been through customs. In his words, it was gone forever. But I had finally arrived in America, and I could always buy a new camera.

*   *   *

My immigration processing at the Ellis Island station took about three hours. I had a work visa and papers showing I had been a U.S. Army contractor, so the procedure was straightforward. The authority filled out the paperwork, gave me two dollars, and said, "Welcome to America."

I boarded a ferry to lower Manhattan, where my friend *Pani* Olenka Kraski met me. She and her husband were living in Manhattan, where they were both working as janitors, even though they were educated people with upper class backgrounds. We had only an hour for a quick reunion before my train left to take me to my new life in Minnesota. *Pani* Olenka wished me well, and told me that she and her husband would be waiting for me if I ended up back in New York.

The train ride west took four days. I was trying to be thrifty, but after a day and a half of eating nothing, I finally went to the dining car and ordered a fifty-cent hamburger. As I waited, I chatted with the waiter about my experiences and plans. When the meal came, it was enormous. I had enough leftovers to wrap and save for the next day.

Eventually I arrived in Winona, Minnesota. It was the middle of December and my God, it was cold! I was met by my new boss, Mr. Terry, and a Catholic priest. This was a relief. I thought to myself, "Well, this may be a whole new world, but at least my new boss is a Catholic." Mr. Terry and I shook hands and he instantly said to the priest, "Father, this can't be the right man. I asked for a mechanic for my service station. Feel his hands—this man is not a manual laborer."

They asked me what kind of work I did. I told them about office work—translating, typing, and running a phone switchboard. I had applied for work as a special services translator. Somehow the consulate must have thought that I wanted to work in a special service station. Mr. Terry said, "Father, it's no use for me to try to train him to work in my garage. It would cost more than I can afford and he'll never be any good at it." I was utterly dismayed. I had arrived at what felt like the middle of nowhere, it was colder than I'd imagined possible, and now I had no job and nowhere to go.

The priest said, "Okay, I will take him to the parish."

Mr. Terry softened and said, "Oh, no, since he's already here, he can stay with us for three weeks."

Mrs. Terry was very gracious. She cooked enormous meals to try and fatten me up. I couldn't eat everything she piled on my plate, which made her worry that I found something wrong with her cooking. I kissed her hand and said, "Mrs. Terry, everything is delightful. I just can't eat this much." I stayed with them while Mr. Terry tried to help me find work. So many GIs were returning from the war and looking for employment that I couldn't get hired anywhere. After the three weeks were up, I told Mr. Terry I had friends in Detroit who might be able to help me find a job there. I promised I would repay him the price of my transportation once I found work. He told me not to worry about it. His two sons had just come back from the war and he viewed my expenses as an offering of thanksgiving for their safe return.

19. Living the American Dream

When I first arrived in the U.S., I had written to my friend from the army office in Giessen, Frieda Lebedinski. She had returned to her family's home in Detroit, and when I wrote to her again to say I was having trouble finding work, she invited me to stay with her family. She lived with her mother and brothers in Detroit. Her father had died of a heart attack during the war. Frieda's brother Henry had fought his way across Europe with the U.S. infantry. Although he and I seldom discussed our wartime experiences, we had an unspoken understanding about them and we became close friends.

Within two days of my arrival in Detroit, Henry found me a job on an auto assembly line. I spent several months helping to install steel plates in the doors of Lincolns and Cadillacs to bullet proof them for politicians and union officials. The job paid fifty cents an hour, which was more than enough to pay Mrs. Lebedinski for my meals, the rent on my attic room, and the bus ticket to get to work. There I was, twenty-three years old, working and saving money. Frieda and I were dating, although most of our dates were walks in the park. I was saving most of my earnings to repay Mr. Terry, despite his objection.

When I moved in with the Lebedinskis, Henry said, "Come on, I'm taking you downtown for some American clothes." He took me to Witkowski's, the best men's clothing store in Hamtramck. I was shocked at the prices. A salesman overheard us talking and came over. Henry told him about me and the salesman said, "Oh, don't worry about the prices. We'll work it out later." I bought everything—shoes, socks, underwear, shirts, and a wool suit. They were all of good quality, and I wore the suit at my wedding five years later. The bill came to $300, although after I took another look at the receipt when I got home, I saw the total was really much more than that. I paid what I could, and Henry loaned me the rest. It wasn't easy to repay him when I was making fifty cents an hour and saving to repay Mr. Terry as well. I often picked up a penny from the shop floor or out of the gutter. Most of the factory guys were careless with their money because they had been there a long time and were making three dollars an hour. They didn't care about pennies, but I sure did.

After a couple of months, Henry told me I would have more opportunity for advancement if I took a different job. He had heard the Plymouth car company in Hamtramck was hiring. It would mean a cut in pay down to twenty-five cents an hour at first, but Henry was sure I would have a better future there and would make more money in the end. That was the plant where the other boys started calling me Limey. I asked someone why and he told me that it was because of my strong English accent. I said, "I'm not English. I'm Polish and proud of it."

The man said, "If you tell them that, they'll call you a dumb Polack. You decide." Okay, Limey it was.

I rode the bus to work on the Plymouth assembly line. On my first day, the boss told me, "Just hang one of these car bodies up every time a hook comes by on the overhead line."

My American co-workers were just screwing around and laughing. After the boss left, they said, "Are you stupid, or what?"

"What's wrong?" I asked.

"You're hanging too many. You'll get us all in trouble."

I said, "Didn't you hear what he said when he came in and told me what to do? You were standing right next to me!"

"Well, so what? You're working too hard and making us look bad." I ignored them and went on hanging up the car bodies.

A couple of hours later, the boss came and stood behind me. Then he yelled at me because some of the hooks were going by empty. "What in the hell did I tell you to do?"

I replied, "I'm doing what you told me."

"No, because look, there go two or three hooks with nothing on them."

I said, "You know what? I'm not the only one who is supposed to be hanging bodies. What about these guys?" The boss looked over to where the other guys were laughing, then he chewed them out for slacking.

Afterwards they were mad at me, cursing and wanting to fight because I had gotten them in trouble. I said, "No, you know it's your own fault. Just leave me alone."

After three months, I got a raise to fifty cents an hour. I told Mrs. Lebedinski and she was very happy for me. She insisted I didn't need to pay her anything extra and that I should just keep working hard. Her two boys had good jobs and Frieda was working as a stenographer. Frieda and I enjoyed being together and we went dancing when I could afford it. I was paying off my debts and starting to save a little—I was living the American dream!

20. The Leland Sanatorium and After

Within six months of starting my job at the Plymouth plant, I developed a high fever and a cough. The veterans' health service diagnosed me with tuberculosis. The doctors there asked me if I had been x-rayed before I came to the U.S. I replied that I had been x-rayed many times and my lungs had always been clear. However, TB was endemic in Europe and its incidence had increased dramatically during the war years when people lacked good food and lived in unsanitary conditions. Although I had been around people with TB many times, I think it got hold of me when I was walking across Germany and surviving on the vegetables I scrabbled out of the frozen fields.

That was the end of my job at the Plymouth plant. I was admitted to the Leland Tuberculosis Sanatorium in Ypsilanti, Michigan. I worried that I would be deported and I am forever grateful to the U.S. government for not shipping me back to Poland. The head nurse at the sanatorium, Miss Frazier, reassured me and told me the government would never send me back, because I had been employed by the U.S. Army.

The treatment was tedious — we all just stayed in bed. I found it a great challenge. Twice a day we got up to march around the ward so we wouldn't lose our muscle tone or get bedsores. Then we returned to our beds and lay still. The chief physician, Dr. Shapiro, said, "Look, Andrew, it's like this. Either you want to get healthy and you cooperate with your treatment, or you can be like a lot of the other guys here and mess around. We can't help them and they stay here until they die. It's up to you."

I said, "I understand. I will do whatever you tell me." I resigned myself to enduring this new way of life. A priest visited us every week, and one of the nurses, Pauline, liked to chat with me. We became good friends and visiting with her helped to pass the time.

During my treatment, Frieda and I drifted apart. I didn't like to expose her to the sanatorium and we both worried that my health was permanently compromised. Frieda decided to return to Europe, where she was hired as a stenographer with the government in Vienna. Her brother Henry visited me every month while I was in the sanatorium. I told him, "Henry, please don't come here. I don't want you to get sick. Your mother needs you," but he was a faithful friend the entire time I was a patient there.

The good food and rest I received at the public health hospital un-doubtedly contributed to my recovery, although I was also subjected to a treatment that did more harm than good. In those days, antibiotic treat-ment for tuberculosis was still in its infancy. At the Leland Sanatorium, the standard, if outdated, therapy was to induce a pneumothorax. This procedure involved collapsing the diseased part of the lung around the infection to encapsulate the infection and prevent the bacilli from spreading. The doctors compressed the lung by injecting nitrogen gas between the chest wall and the lung. One of the physicians at the sana-torium was an elderly Army doctor named Dr. Wright. He had no bed-side manner or rapport with his patients, and treated us as annoyances rather than as humans. Worse, he was an alcoholic and he argued con-stantly with the head nurse, Miss Frazier. She had been a public health nurse since World War I and she knew her job. Even the patients could hear her calling Dr. Wright a drunken son of a bitch who should be kicked out of the hospital. She hated assisting him when he performed the pneumothorax procedure because she knew how dangerous the op-eration could be, especially when carried out by a shaky-handed drunk.

When the time came for my procedure, Dr. Wright stuck the needle in my ribs and I heard him tell the nurse to open the machine and turn on the pressure. Then I lost consciousness. When I came to, I had an unbearable headache — and I was totally blind.

I was in shock. My head hurt so much I couldn't think. I was terrified that I would spend the rest of my life alone in an asylum for the blind and insane. I felt a little better after the chief physician examined me. I remember Dr. Shapiro's voice clearly, because I clung to his words for any sign of hope. He said, "Andrew, you will be okay. You will get better. Try not to worry." Dr. Shapiro's calm and competent manner gave me some confidence that I would recover. He told the nurses to keep me sitting upright and not to let me move until the next day.

Despite his reassurance, Dr. Shapiro was very concerned about my case. My friend Pauline told me later that he instructed the nurses who came to my room to stop in the doorway and assess my reaction — to see if I could recognize people before they spoke to me. The nurses came often and even though I couldn't see them, I could always recognize them by the sounds of their movements and their voices. Providentially, after a few days, my vision began to clear. Dr. Shapiro came in and asked if I could see anything. I replied that I could see his fingers moving. What a relief! He told me not to worry, that I would recover, and thanks be to God, my sight did indeed return to normal over the next several weeks.

Meanwhile, Dr. Wright injured two other veterans with the same pneumothorax procedure. They had contracted tuberculosis while serving in Korea. Dr. Wright's treatment permanently blinded them. Their parents and a veterans group filed complaints for them and Dr. Wright was dismissed. Miss Frazier felt vindicated. She told me, "At last I got what I wanted. He's gone and I can go home at night and not worry about all the harm he's doing."

I spent three years in the sanatorium. It was not a bad place, except for the monotony of lying in bed all day. The windows looked out into a pine forest and they were kept open day and night so we always had fresh air. Even in the winter, the windows were cracked open and we lay with blankets up to our chins. Nurses put clean sheets on our beds every day and the food was nutritious, with lots of eggs and custards. The antibiotic Mycitracin was just being introduced and it worked well in my case, so that eventually I made a complete recovery. Others were less fortunate. The ward next to mine housed the hopeless cases. Pauline asked me if I would shave some of the men in the terminal ward. She told me I needed to wear a surgical mask while I shaved them so I wouldn't be exposed to new germs. I said, "Pauline, how could I hurt their feelings by letting them think I am afraid of them? I will shave them, but I won't wear the mask."

Pauline said, "Well, I'll have to talk to Miss Frazier to get permission for that." Miss Frazier told me that if I was careful and washed with antiseptic soap, I would be okay. I shaved a few of the dying men and some of them shaved each other. I still think of those helpless guys lying there with death sentences.

*   *   *

After my eventual discharge from the sanatorium, I needed to find another job and a place to live. I didn't want to go back to Mrs. Lebedinski's house, because I worried I might bring contagion with me. A social worker named Mrs. Osbourne told me that if I couldn't find a place, I would be committed to an asylum. I said, "Well, you better just put a bullet in my head right now, because I'm not going to an asylum."

Mrs. Osbourne helped me find a place with a family who had a room to rent. She also found me a job with an optician who trained me in fitting and adjusting glasses. Optical work suited me because I had both the dexterity to work with delicate instruments and the patience to make repeated adjustments. I also liked working with our clients. I especially enjoyed fitting glasses for cloistered nuns who could not leave their convents. They lived lives of simplicity and prayer, but they still needed to see. Many people seemed to enjoy telling me their stories, and I found their accounts of American life fascinating. People can always tell if you are genuinely interested in them.

Every month I had to go back to the sanatorium for a chest x-ray, but my lungs remained clear. The doctors told me to take it easy and just go to work and then rest—no late nights of drinking and carousing, or I'd have a relapse. That gave me a strong incentive to behave.

Despite spending three years on hold, I felt optimistic. I was once again making my own way in my new country. With steady work, I finally repaid my debts and began saving money for myself. I also met the girl I would marry. Her name was Mary Lou Lederman. She and I became acquainted through friends at church. We discovered through our early conversations that we were seeking similar qualities in a life-partner—faith, commitment to family, and a strong work ethic. Mary Lou came from a large family, and she taught music and mathematics in the Detroit Catholic school system. I was charmed by her love of music. She played the piano beautifully, and we enjoyed going dancing together.

Mary Lou and I married in 1953 and her aunt sold us a small house in the Detroit suburb of Ferndale. Our two sons were born into the

America of the 1950's. I am thankful that they have never had to live in a world consumed by war.

I became a U.S. citizen in 1958. As soon as we could afford it, I began helping my Polish family emigrate to America. The process was hindered by Cold War enmity between the U.S. and the Soviet Union. However, with the support of my congressional delegation, my mother, sisters, and niece were able to join my family in Detroit by the mid 1960's. Maria's friend Bernard was also able to emigrate to the U.S. He settled in New Jersey and he and Maria carried on a long-distance relationship for many years, although they never married.

I carried my life-long love of the forest and wildlife in my heart and found city life in Detroit confining. Mary Lou and I saved until we could buy property "up north," as they say in Michigan. We built a lake-front house and invested in a Dairy Queen franchise in the resort town of Houghton Lake. My mother and sisters worked at the Dairy Queen, Mary Lou found a teaching job nearby, I found a new optometrist to work for, and we were able to leave Detroit behind. One of the first things I planted at our new home was a linden tree, so that we could enjoy the scent of the blossoms we remembered from Poland.

*   *   *

My mother and sisters lived with us for the rest of their lives. Mother lived to the age of 101. Mary Lou passed away in 2016. One of my sons lives nearby while the other lives in the Pacific Northwest. I work in my garden in the summer and I tend my fire in the winter. Life is what it is.

The tolerance, thankfulness, and generosity my grandfather taught me have carried me on a long road from a farm in rural Poland, through the conflagration of an evil war, to my garden in northern Michigan. I think about the vanished way of life *Dziadzia* led as a boy in the Poland of 1850 and I cannot imagine the life my newly-born great-granddaughter will have. My own life has been like a bubble on a river. Time carries everyone down that river, sometimes through peaceful sunlit meadows and sometimes through wild and terrifying rapids. Other people come and go around us like bubbles that appear and disappear, winking in the sun.

Appendix:

Guide to Polish Pronunciation

Polish people address one another as *Pan* (Mister or Sir, for men and older boys) and *Pani* (Missus or Lady, for ladies and older girls). Last names that end in *–ski* for a male will end in *–ska* for a female, since they are adjectival endings. In Polish, adjectives agree with a noun's gender.

At first glance, reading and pronouncing Polish words and names can look daunting. However, most letters and letter "clusters" consistently correspond to specific sounds. Breaking a word into syllables and remembering the pronunciation of the various letter clusters makes pronouncing Polish straight-forward, although still demanding. The Polish alphabet also contains nine letters with diacritical marks that affect their pronunciation.

Pronunciation guide to some of the Polish
words and names used in this book

Andrzej	AHN-zhay	Andrew
Babcia	BAHB-chah	Grandmother
Basia	BAH-shah	Barbara
Bujakiewicz	Boo-yah-kee-YEH-vich	My grandfather's surname
Biszek	BEE-shek	A surname
Chumiętki	Khoom-i-YENT-kee	Name of nearby estate
Ciocia	CHO-chah	Aunt
Dzienki bogu	JEN-kee BOH-goo	Thanks be to God
Dziadzia	Jah-Jah	Grandfather
Dzień dobry	Jin DOH-brih	Good morning
Frusia	FROO-sha	Kathy
Gwiazdor	GVYAHZ-door	Star-man, Santa Claus
Kasia	KAH-shah	Kathy
Kokoszki	Koh-KOH-shkee	Hamlet at Pudliszki gates
Krobia	KROH-byuh	My home town
Jolanta	Yoh-LAHN-tah	Yolanda
Jurek	YUR-eck	George
Jurkowski	Yur-KOFF-skee	My surname
Nusia	NOO-sha	Woman's name
Pudliszki	Pud-LISH-kee	Name of estate and factory
Pułkownik	Puy-KOH-vnik	Colonel
Przywara	Pzheh-VAH-rah	A surname
Ratusz	RAH-toosh	City Hall
Slawa	SLAH-vah	Woman's name
Stanislaw	STAN-is-swahv	Man's name
Tadeusz	Tah-DAY-oosh	Thadeus

Walenty	Vah-WEN-tee	Valentine
Waleria	Vah-LAIR-ee-yah	Valerie
Wigilia	Vih-JEEEL-yah	Christmas Eve vigil dinner
Wladyslaw	VWAHD-i-swahv	Man's name
Wlady	VWAHD-ee	Nickname for Wladyslaw
Wojciech	VOY-chek	Man's name
Wujo	VOO-yoh	Uncle
Zofia	Zoh-FEE-yah	Sophia
Zosia	ZOH-shah	Sophie

Acknowledgements

I am profoundly grateful for the support Réanne Hemingway Douglass and her husband Don Douglass gave me during the writing of this book. Réanne's interest in publishing accounts of civilian life during World War II encouraged me to bring Andrew's stories from a much-discussed concept to realization. Don and Réanne generously allowed me to write this book while working on other projects at Cave Art Press.

I owe a great debt to Arlene Cook for her patient editing and meticulous fact-checking. Her organizational skills created a semblance of order out of the chaos of my manuscript. All remaining errors are my sole responsibility.

Family discussions of the people and events of Polish history in general, and Andrew's life in particular, helped shaped this narrative. I am also grateful to my manuscript readers for their encouragement and suggestions. Thanks to Robert Wright, D.Z. Stone, Nicholas Jurkowski, Donna Kleppin, Kathleen Kaska, and Réanne Hemingway-Douglass.

As always, my husband, daughter, and son supplied their invaluable common sense and support throughout this process. Thank you.

Lisa Wright

Made in the USA
Columbia, SC
22 September 2018